A child prodigy of the violin, t
introduced to the instrument a
professional recital when she was only seven. So impressed was her
compatriot, Emil Telmanyi, by her playing that he arranged for her to
study at the Royal Academy in Budapest, where she received the
traditional Hungarian virtuoso training. Later, she toured most of
the major European capitals, made her Carnegie Hall debut at
seventeen and was acclaimed by the critics everywhere.

Whereas most child prodigies find a period of retirement essential if
they are to achieve maturity of mind and musicianship, with Kato
Havas, this happened quite naturally. She married at eighteen and,
while bringing up her three daughters, withdrew altogether from
professional life. It was during this period of withdrawal that she
developed her revolutionary method of teaching. In pondering the
questions and limitations of contemporary violin playing, she found
that she had stumbled upon the core of the problem. She began to
teach a few people, mostly friends, and the results were so startling
and instantaneous that, as soon as her daughters were at boarding
school, she began to give lessons seriously.

In the early sixties, a series of articles about her method by Noel
Hale F.R.A.M. appeared in *The Strad*. "I was privileged", wrote
Hale, "to witness the teaching of a method of violin playing entirely
new to me, which I believe is capable of revolutionizing the technique
of playing . . . writing as a personal witness, I must say that I have
been amazed at the results of this unusual approach."

Miss Havas was invited to lecture at Oxford; she gave talks and
demonstrations on television. Over the years, she has given a series of
lecture demonstrations in Great Britain, Australia, New Zealand,
Canada and in many European countries. She has travelled
extensively in the United States giving workshops at major
universities on the release of tension and anxiety in violin and viola
playing. She was the founder and Director of the Purbeck Festival of
Music, the Roehampton Music Festival and the International
Festival in Oxford, where she is now based. Players come to her from
all over the world.

In 1992, the American String Teachers' Association conferred upon
her its prestigious International Award in recognition of her
"unparalleled achievements".

Kato Havas's books have so far been translated into German,
Swedish, Spanish, Czech and Chinese.

STAGE FRIGHT

STAGE FRIGHT

its

Causes and Cures

With Special Reference to Violin Playing

by

KATO HAVAS

BOSWORTH & Co. Ltd.

Dedication

To Tim for his kindness and understanding in having a violinist for a wife, and to Sue, Pam and Kate for their sense of humour and forbearance in having a violinist for a mother.

Acknowledgements

I would like to express my gratitude to Dr. F. A. Hellebrandt, Professor Emeritus, University of Wisconsin, formerly Director of the Motor Learning Research Laboratory, School of Medicine and Education, Wisconsin, for making clear the scientific aspects of *A New Approach to Violin Playing* and *The Twelve Lesson Course* in a series of articles in *The Strad*, in private correspondence and in many discussions. Any misinterpretations in this book of Dr. Hellebrandt's ideas are entirely my own. I would also like to thank Rosemary Manning and Veldes Raison for their helpful and constructive criticism during the preparation of this book, and the many violinists from all corners of the world who enabled me to write it.

Drawings by Nicholas Thorne

Contents

Introduction

Although I did not know it at the time, the seeds of this book were sown when I was seven.

A first recital is always a big event, especially if one happens to be seven years old. I clearly remember the pink rococo-style taffeta frock with the matching bow in my hair and the two things that were dinned into me. The first was that I should look on the audience as if they were so many cabbages and on no account was I to take any notice of them. The second was that I should go on playing no matter what happened.

The cabbage idea I did not understand at all. Why should I turn the audience into cabbages when I could hardly wait to play for them? So the moment I stepped on stage and heard the applause I forgot all thoughts of cabbages, and I remember to this day the face of the woman in the front row. But I followed the second idea and when, due to a short circuit, all the lights went out (the performance took place in Transylvania), I dutifully continued with the fast 'tee-tee-tuum-tum-um-pa-papapapapa-pum' bit of the Brahms Hungarian Dances, even though the pianist did not.

By the age of fourteen, however, I knew better, and at my first recital in Budapest (at the Academy of Music) I would have given a pretty penny for the audience to turn into cabbages, especially when at the beginning of the *Devil's Trill* I saw Hubay, Kodaly, Weiner, Dohnanyi, and Bartok appear, one by one, on the balcony level with the stage. They had come to find out what the girl from Transylvania sounded like. Hubay with his long white hair and white beard not only resisted all ideas of turning into a cabbage, but looked like a dignitary from Heaven itself, ready to dole out the most terrifying punishment. So all I could do was lose awareness, and all I remember is coming to only at the sound of applause at the end.

By the age of seventeen, at my debut in Carnegie Hall in New York, I not only knew that the cabbage idea was useless, but I also knew that one cannot lose awareness at will. What saved me was the heat, the tropical, steambath kind of heat, which only New York can produce, although it was October. I was too busy trying to stay alive to worry about anything else.

However, I also learned from my short but intensive career between the ages of seven and seventeen, that stage fright was something completely unpredictable. It would come and shake one to the core at the most unexpected moments, in tiny concert halls, in unimportant places, and yet when most expected, it might remain absent.

During the subsequent tours and orchestral appearances I also discovered that, with or without stage fright, no praise, no wonderful review on earth could make me feel happy if I myself did not feel happy with my playing. In fact, praise could make me feel even more miserable. It seemed that the only thing that mattered in my playing was me. Violin playing was a lonely life, and I was convinced that ordinary life was passing me by. I decided that the only solution was to opt out and get married. I was eighteen.

However, the ensuing lull provided the most important period in my whole career. It gave me time to think and to discover some answers to the difficulties besetting so many violinists. And when, eighteen years later, fate decided virtually to 'rocket' me back to the musical world (see *The Violin and I*), I knew that the misery so many violinists experience was totally unnecessary.

But the alleviation of stage fright was still an enigma. That was to come after the publication of three books, ten years of intensive teaching, constant public lecture demonstrations on both sides of the Atlantic, plus the running of my Summer Violin School and Festival.

'During this period of work . . . I discovered an additional result of the New Approach—the alleviating of stage fright.' These lines were written in 1967 in an autobiographical account called *The Violin and I*. The book describes the origins and consequent developments of a method of violin teaching, which I called *A New Approach to*

Violin Playing. The reason for calling this method a 'New Approach' was that instead of following the conventional methods of violin teaching, it was based on the fundamental principles of co-ordinated balances.

In order to simplify the scientific terminology of the physiological key motor responses, I had referred to them in my previous two books, *A New Approach to Violin Playing* and *The Twelve Lesson Course in Violin Playing*, as the 'Fundamental Balances'. In other words, in order to release (and in the case of beginners to avoid) tension and anxiety, so often a part of violin playing, the pupil learns to apply effortless, natural, body-motions, as in rowing, swimming or playing tennis, instead of the traditional 'placing', (very often actually forcing) of the body and hands. These co-ordinated self-propelled physical actions naturally tend to evoke great release in the emotional and mental responses.

The 'period of work' I referred to above culminated in a recital in the Wigmore Hall, arranged by Messrs. Bosworth and Co. Ltd., to launch the publication of my second book, *The Twelve Lesson Course in a New Approach to Violin Playing*.

The reason for arranging the recital was to show the results obtainable through this method of teaching. The pupils taking part were aged from seven to fifty-five and their skill was equally varied. From beginner to professional, all were represented, including amateurs, students and teachers. The duration of their studies with me also varied to the extreme, from twelve lessons to three years.

It was on this occasion that I was amazed to see that some of these pupils, although they had had no more than twelve lessons in their lives, had never played in front of even a roomful of people before, let alone a jammed audience at the Wigmore Hall, showed no sign of nerves from the moment they began to play.

But what interested me, especially at this recital, was the reaction of the professional players. Most of them had suffered agonies of stage fright at previous public appearances and these had affected their playing to such a degree that one or two of them were seriously thinking of giving up playing in public altogether. But on this occasion all of them, without exception, were not only free from nerves, but positively enjoyed the sensation of playing in front of an audience. For the first time in their lives they were able to taste the intoxicating feeling of artistic fulfilment—the power to 'give'

'There is still much to be learned about the nature of stage fright', I wrote in *The Violin and I*. 'What causes it? What are the physical manifestations? Why are certain people more affected than others? These and other questions are the core to which we hope to find some positive answers and solutions in the course of time.' I felt very strongly that the results at that concert in the Wigmore Hall were only a beginning.

Therefore, I began to make a special study of the causes and effects relating to stage fright. And because of the nature of my work, which has always involved me with players of all standards, I had ample opportunity to observe and to make notes. It proved to be a most complex and absorbing study, involving physiology, psychology and sociology.

Through these studies, much research, and through constant public appearances, I have had the good fortune to amass a vast amount of experience on the subject. Also, working with so many players, I have had enough opportunity of expanding and developing the concepts and techniques for the release from tension and anxiety, and thus of adding further curative measures specific to stage fright. The response exceeded all my expectations. And when at the Mannes School of Music in New York practically the whole audience lined up to get first-hand experience on the point in question, I was forced to remind them that they were attending a lecture demonstration and not a Billy Graham meeting. It was this overwhelming response to the possible alleviation of stage fright which met me on every occasion, that finally decided me to put my findings down on paper.

Most of the training on how to release tension and anxiety which I am going to discuss in the following chapters, applies to all performers on any instrument. But as the problems of violinists tend to be more complex than most, because of the very nature of the instrument, and because theirs is the world I know best, I am going to single out the violin for the purpose of this book.

The clarifications involve the understanding of the origins and causes of the problems. This understanding involves both physical and mental training. It entails the re-education of our attitudes to the physical movements in handling an instrument. It involves understanding what communicative music-making consists of and what artist-audience relationship is all about. And now, after years of constant testing and observation I feel justified in stating that with training, understanding and application, stage fright can in fact be cured.

So I am really back where I was at the age of seven. But what I only sensed then, now I know—that there is no such joy in the whole world as when one can 'give' to an audience without the burden of stage fright. I only hope that through this book my long road of experience may prove to be of some help to my fellow violinists.

I

A General Survey

1. The shame attached to stage fright

Stage fright is one of the most destructive elements in the performing arts, be it acting, dancing, singing, making a speech, or playing an instrument.

As Dr Deri, the musicologist, says in his paper, 'Stage Fright— The Musician's No. 1 Enemy':

> Among all anxieties accompanying public performances, the fear that grips the concert artist, seems to outrank all others . . . the words of a young musician may bring the following home: "The platform does something to me. The vacuum up there seems to suck the marrow out of my bones, to numb my fingers and worst of all, to put my memory out of commission." The worst aspect of stage fright is that once its paralysing force has been experienced, it tends to leave a lasting impression.

What is more, to most performers nerves represent some sort of terrible and personal shortcoming. In most cases stage fright is considered shameful, a kind of degrading disease, something akin to leprosy which is best kept a dark secret.

> The idea of faulty behaviour is a personal misfortune and often leads to the conclusion that it must be covered up. The result is that the majority present outwardly a veneer designed to cover up all short-comings.*

Of course, when one achieves stardom it is easier to confess to nerves. But even then this is mostly true in the world of ballet and theatre. On the whole, musicians, even the great ones, are apt to be ashamed of it. This is especially true of violinists.

This sense of shame originates in very deep-rooted insecurities, both physical and psychological, which produce major problems for most players.

The reasons for these deep-rooted anxieties are manifold, but the major cause is that few violinists are able to achieve even a tolerable, let alone an active, feeling of physical confidence during a performance. The discomfort of an aching back or hands often goes with traditional violin training.

Body and Mature Behaviour by M. Feldenkrais International Universities Press Inc., New York, 1949

2

> The Violinist must take the greatest care of his finger-tips . . . removing the callous skin with scissors may cause permanent injury . . . the irritation may be diminished by covering temporarily the tip with a finger guard of soft kid. . . . Frequent and even permanent *muscular pains* in the arm may be fought by health treatment or by massage. Sometimes the tonsils may be responsible for it. One should not hesitate to apply to a specialist for advice.*

The remedies for 'sore inflamed places and abscesses' and for the 'cramped contraction of the ball of the thumb' I have already quoted in my *New Approach To Violin Playing* on pages 8 and 10, and I will not go into them here. But it seems quite obvious that in those days doctors were kept as busy with violinist patients as physiotherapists are today.

These physical discomforts and the effort of tackling difficult passages under these conditions, are enough to handicap, if not totally to prevent, the release of the artistic flow even in the most talented player, and as the flow of communication is the most essential factor for a successful performance, it is small wonder that most players would go to any length in order to cover up the mental and physical frustrations of not being able to 'give'. Needless to say, some players (depending on the degree of their physical ease and mental discipline) are able partially or wholly to overcome these discomforts during a performance. But these break-throughs are usually sporadic and few players can rely on them.

Kreisler was one of the very few violinists I myself have heard, who not only managed to create an aura of magic from beginning to end during a performance, but who seemed totally oblivious of stage fright. A great many stories circulated about Kreisler, before and after his death, and one. of them is that he never practised. I will return to the 'Kreisler phenomenon' later, in the chapter dealing with methods of practising. However, I have often witnessed his complete disregard of stresses and strains on the platform, and what looked like a marvellous disregard for his violin as well.

However, whether it was his ability to create continuous and sheer magic which made stage fright non-existent for him, or whether

---

The Art of Violin Playing, by Carl Flesch, New York, 1930.

because he was not suffering from stage fright, he could, in fact, create magic, is a question I would like to bring up later in connection with the Hungarian gypsy violinists.

The best example of another aspect of extreme physical skill and mental discipline was Heifetz. Many people, for all their admiration, considered him cold as a person and as a violinist. However, if one understands the reasons that lie behind stage fright, where it originates, why it exists, one understands that the coldness and absolute technical precision amounted to nothing more than an enormous, accumulated discipline which in time developed into a kind of protective veneer. This, of course, applies to a great many violinists in differing degrees.

There is an interesting and revealing article on Heifetz in his retirement, by an American journalist, Roger Kahn, called 'Fiddler on the Shelf'.* Among other things there was an account of his playing with the Israeli Philharmonic Orchestra, and according to the article, as Heifetz started towards the stage entrance, Tatiana, his housekeeper, saw a face which looked 'stricken with fright'. Impulsively, a devout Greek Orthodox believer, she clutched Heifetz's arm and stroked it. 'God will look after you,' she promised. 'After Heifetz fiddled triumphantly through the last movement, a woman seated next to Tatiana in a box embraced her not knowing who she was, and cried at the beauty of what she heard.' This just goes to show that if the skill coupled with the desire to 'give' is great enough, it can overcome all the destructive elements of stage fright. But is it possible for all violinists to develop sufficient skill with sufficient desire to 'give' when confronted with an audience?

Life Magazine, Oct. 31, 1969.

4

2. The symptoms of stage fright

One thing is certain. Nobody plays the same way in front of an audience as when alone within the privacy of his own four walls, be the audience three people or three thousand. One either plays much better or much worse—alas, more often than not, much worse.

It is important to understand that all of us, each single human being, even if he is not an actor, dancer, musician or violinist, and has only an undemanding job, is endowed with a fair share of anxiety. According to many psychologists, anxiety does not only exist in every human being, but it is a very necessary part of his psychic make-up.

> Man, being both bound and free, both limited and limitless, is anxious. Anxiety is the inevitable concomitant of the paradox of freedom and finiteness in which man is involved.*

The continuous need to overcome anxiety creates a certain driving force in the human being which is generally considered healthy and good. It is only when a person is incapable of overcoming his anxiety that neurosis sets in.

Stage fright is nothing more nor less than an exaggerated symptom of anxiety. Heifetz, to return to him, could always handle it, and so can many others in differing degrees. But in the majority of cases, the devastation of stage fright is merciless. It leaves a wake of desolation, both physical and mental, not to talk of the horrors of artistic frustration.

> No one has described fully the horror of this illness called anxiety. Worse than any physical illness, is this illness of the soul, for it is insidious, elusive and arouses no pity. †

Almost fifty years have passed since Freud announced that all emotional and behavioural disorders stem from the central point of anxiety, and the opinion that anxiety is the dynamic centre of neurosis has not altered significantly up to this date.

*The Nature and Destiny of Man, by Reinhold Niebuhr, Chas. Scribner and Sons, New York, 1941.

†The Journals of Anais Nin, Peter Owen, London, 1966.

This dynamic centre of neurosis when manifested in stage fright hits one like a disease. It affects the whole body though the actual symptoms vary with each individual. The hands become either icy cold in the hottest climate, or damp with sweat in an ice-cold room. One is either yawning all the time, or one's throat is so dry that it is difficult to swallow. Nausea, or the inability to eat and the need to relieve oneself seem to be the most common and universal symptoms. However, the power of anxiety is so fundamental and its symptoms are so varied that it is impossible to pin them down to one single cause. The causes seem to fall into three categories: physical, mental and social.

But before going any further it is important to clarify the difference between fear and anxiety.

> The central difference between fear and anxiety is that fear is a reaction to a specific danger, while anxiety is unspecific, 'vague', 'objectless'. The special characteristics of anxiety are the feeling of *uncertainty* and *helplessness* in the face of danger.*

The danger, in the case of a recital, is the recital itself. The player is afraid to go out to face the audience because he has a feeling of helplessness and uncertainty (anxiety) about doing justice to his artistic abilities. Will he play well? Will the performance be a success or a failure? These feelings of acute fear and anxiety apply especially to soloists at the all-important event of their lives—the debut. In the case of orchestra players, chamber musicians and opera singers, the anxiety tends to be less unbearable, because a certain amount of team work is involved and the need to sustain their performance without interruption is somewhat diminished. In the case of actors it is even easier because there is constant interdependence among the performers. In the theatre world there exists the opportunity for most plays to be tried out in the provinces which allows the actors both to overcome their possible shortcomings, and to prepare themselves for the first night in the capital. In the case of a young musician, because of the way in which musical careers are shaped in our present social system, no one will give him a tour unless he is already successful; therefore, not only does he

---

*The Meaning of Anxiety, by Rollo May, The Ronald Press Company, New York, 1950.

6

have to find money to finance the first all-important event, his debut, but his whole future may depend upon the success of it. The stronger this fear of the outcome of his performance is allowed to be, the more exaggerated the anxiety becomes, with all its disastrous effects on body and mind.

> The nature of anxiety can be understood when we ask *what* is threatened in the experience which produces anxiety. The threat is to something in the 'core or essence' of the personality. *Anxiety is the apprehension cued off by a threat to some value* which the individual holds essential to his existence as a personality.*

In the case of a solo performer, the threat refers to his 'success' around which most of his life revolves.

With violinists the anxiety for 'success' tends to become even more exaggerated than with other performers. The technical problems are often present even without an audience: the trembling right arm during slow strokes; misjudging the shifts to high positions; the seizing up of the left hand in fast passages; the slowness of vibrato; double stops, trills and intonation, just to name a few of the ever-present difficulties.

For instance, I find, after working with hundreds of players, the most deeply hidden, the most common and the most shame-making fear is that of dropping the violin. In fact, I have found that this particular problem is very often at the root of all other difficulties, and is, of course, unique to violinists and violists.

It is interesting to note how many disappointed violinists turn to playing the viola as a last resort because they think that the viola might be easier to handle. But of course this is far from the truth. If anything, the problems become even more exaggerated because of its very size. Otherwise why are there no notable viola soloists, with the exception of one or two international names? And why is there no more literature written for the viola? It is a lovely instrument with a gorgeous sound. But technical anxieties, including the actual fear that the instrument will fall unless one grabs it (especially during shifts to high positions) are considerably increased.

No wonder that both violinists and violists tend to become irritable and miserable days before the dreaded event of an audition

Ibid.

7

or examination. Also, no wonder that they are reluctant to pick up their violins and 'play' especially when asked to play for Auntie May to show their prowess. The fear of 'exposure' is too unbearable to face.

These fears which are rooted in unreliable physical actions are enough to cast a permanent shadow over the lives of many violinists. But even when this is not the case, because the player's technical proficiency is so natural and effortless that he has no cause to fear, there is another deep-rooted anxiety, so strong that it tends to overshadow all other assets of technical proficiency. It stems from a subconscious fear that 'if I don't do well nobody will love me'. It goes back to early childhood when one's whole existence evolved around being loved. It is a pernicious anxiety especially prevalent among highly-strung, precocious children, and it is one of the major causes for stage fright later on in life.

3. *Artist-audience relationship*

If violinists were encouraged or, indeed, were allowed, to look on themselves as artists and creative artists at that—from their student days onward—many of the destructive elements of stage fright could be eliminated from the beginning.

Most people agree that what separates an artist from the rest of humanity is the fact that the artist is endowed with a heightened degree of sensitivity, awareness and imagination, and that the significance of each individual artist depends entirely on the degree of his ability to impart to his fellow humans this heightened perception, be it visual or aural.

The idea of 'limitless human potential' goes way back to Greek mythology—'the god-like men and the man-like gods'. Or to the concept of Christianity—'We are all built in the image of God'. Every human being has a divine spark, says Emerson, it is only a question of how to develop it into a flaming torch. And who better than an artist can enable his fellow creatures to be lifted out of their everyday existence and become aware of their divine inheritance? Whether it is Rembrandt or Picasso, Beethoven or Bartok, the power of communication is such that it can influence a multitude of people for many hundreds of years.

The same thing applies to performers as well, especially nowadays when recording has given the performance to posterity. Often one sees tired, sad, sometimes frightened expressions on people's faces among a concert audience, only to encounter the same people again at the end of a memorable performance, with shining eyes and beautiful smiling faces. There is no doubt that at such times a wonderful transformation has taken place. The artist has 'communicated'.

The question is why does this phenomenon happen so seldom? What happens to the majority of the great talents? What becomes of many of the brilliantly promising careers? Why are most of the products of great schools and great masters not among the brightly shining stars at the top? Indeed, why are there, in every generation, only a handful of really great players, after so many distinguished beginnings? 'Alas,' says Liszt in his book *The Gipsy in Music*,* bemoaning the over-emphasis on the mechanical virtuosity in the concertizing world instead of an integral artistry . . . 'such powers are not acquired, being only exercised by right divine.'

The trouble is, that because of the demands of 'success' from early childhood onward, the 'right divine' seldom has a chance to develop, let alone reach fulfilment. Beset with accumulated technical difficulties, examinations, international competitions, the positive side of music-making, the over-riding desire to communicate, soon gives way to anxieties and fears. 'Will I succeed at the audition?' 'Will the great man teach me?' 'Will I win the first prize and thus become known overnight?' It is almost inevitable that by the time a student reaches maturity, the importance and the constant evaluation of his own self become the dominant factors in his career—and stop him from fulfilling his potential of the 'right divine'.

The whole concert world is so impregnated with continuous self-justification and competitive behaviour patterns that it affects the audience as well. We all know that the public has been conditioned, through generations, to criticize and judge, much more than to enjoy. Heifetz himself was convinced that at every performance he gave, two thousand nine hundred and ninety-nine people out of three thousand had come to hear him play a wrong note.

*William Reeves, London, 1926.

9

So, even if the artist is not hindered by stage fright, more often than not his communicating impulse is blocked by the public itself. In order to achieve a real sense of enjoyment on both sides of the lights, his desire to 'give' ought to be met with a desire to 'receive' on the part of the audience. Sometimes the artist is obliged to get half way through the performance before he manages to break through the traditional barrier between him and his public. If he also happens to be plagued with even a few destructive symptoms of stage fright, he considers himself lucky to get through the notes without any major disaster.

It is interesting to note the difference in the over-all impression made by a concert audience and a theatre audience in their respective foyers before a performance. The latter creates an atmosphere of festivity, expectancy and elegance. The people in theatres are obviously out to enjoy themselves. They may not like the play; they may be disappointed in the performance of one of the cast; they are by no means without critical faculties; but first and foremost they are out to have a good time. Concert audiences, on the other hand, tend to look rather serious with an intellectual aura about them, especially when they are also equipped with impressive-looking scores. The excitement and expectancy tend to come to the fore only when somebody like Rubinstein or Rostrapovitch is to appear. Whether it is the inability of most performers to communicate which conditions the audience to its severe outlook, or whether its very severity stops the desire to communicate, is the same enigma as that of the chicken and the egg. Which was created first? Though one would imagine that if more players could 'give', the audience would be more ready to 'receive'.

Liszt of course was right. Artists, like poets, are born, not made. But it is also true that physical and mental blockages can reduce the artistic impulses (impulses equal, perhaps, to those of Oistrakh or Menuhin) to such a degree that after a period of time they become completely atrophied.

Therefore, the work lies in creating a network of channels through which the player can transmit his potential flow of communication, *in spite of* the difficulties surrounding him. Naturally the potential varies to an enormous degree. But there *is* a potential in everybody.

II

The Hungarian Gypsy Violinist

When working on the problems of stage fright, it is inevitable, (especially to a Hungarian) for the question to arise: why don't the gypsy violinists suffer from it? Why are they free to play the most difficult technical passages with such complete ease on any violin and under any circumstances? Why can they produce a tone with all the colours of the rainbow in it? Why are they able to put one through a vast range of emotional experiences at the drop of a hat? Of course the reasons are manifold. First of all they are not burdened with the responsibilities of our social system. They do not have to be better than their fellows in order to succeed. In fact, they would be hard pressed to understand why anybody wants to succeed at all. Secondly, their sole interest is the pleasure of the listeners. They are free from all obligations, except the one and only obligation—to communicate.

Anybody who has heard a real country gypsy play the violin knows that the quality of his tone with its infinite haunting variety, his incredible rhythmic pulse, his almost devilish technical facility, rank him among the few top violinists in the world; and his ability to become one with his listener is phenomenal. There is a Hungarian proverb that the Magyar peasant becomes intoxicated on a glass of water when a gypsy fiddler plays for him.

Professor Starkie's wonderful little book *Raggle-Taggle* describes one of the best encounters with the gypsy phenomenon. His first meeting with them was in a prisoner-of-war camp after the First World War, where he was asked if he could arrange for them to have some wooden boxes. 'Why?' asked Starkie. 'So we can make violins out of them' came the answer. Later on, when Starkie lived among them in Hungary, he noted that often the wandering gypsy didn't even have a case in which to pack his violin. It was strung on his back in a shabby old bag with the bow protruding from the top. 'Pathetic sights they were, those poor Transylvanian fiddles,' he says with feeling. 'They had been for many years subjected to every change of weather—and yet those poor instruments, when touched by the thyrsus of the God of rhythm, respond as if they possessed in the grain of their wood a particle of that magic which gave to the Cremonas their golden tone.'*

Among the great musicians fascinated by the phenomenal artistry of the gypsy, was Liszt. He too lived among them for long periods of time and their influence on him, both as a composer and as a performer, was very considerable indeed. The following extract from one of his letters to a gypsy friend gives a good picture of his attitude to them.

> I almost envy you for having escaped from the civilized art of music-making, with its limitations and crampings. . . . No prattle and jargon from pedants, cavillers and critics and all the nameless brood of such can reach you. . . . Yes my dear Jozsy, you have done well not to engage in concert-room torture, and to disdain the empty, painful reputation of a *thorough* violinist. . . . †

Now, of course, for most of us 'thorough' violinists it would be totally impracticable, if not altogether impossible, to discard our social inheritance and become like the gypsies; refuse to take examinations, enter competitions, and give auditions. So the question is, what *can* we learn from them that would help prevent and eliminate stage fright?

The first thing that comes to mind is the ease with which they handle their instruments, from the word go. For example, while

---

Raggle Taggle, by Walter Starkie, John Murray, London, 1933.
†*The Gipsy in Music*, by Franz Liszt, William Reeves, London.

13

most of us classical violinists just about manage, after years of hard work, to establish a sort of love-hate relationship with our violins, the gypsy's unadulterated pleasure in merely handling the instrument is a joy to watch. He conveys a feeling of not playing on the instrument, but of playing *through* it (see *The Violin and I*, pp. 18-20). While a 'thorough' violinist is often acutely uncomfortable (if not in actual physical pain), the gypsy's bodily well-being, as he plays his instrument, is unassailable. If he saw the stacks of exercises and studies compulsory to a classical violinist, he would run a mile; and if he were asked to go through the same physical rigidities as many of us do, he would laugh at the suggestion—or would stop playing altogether. With us, physical rigidity is such an accepted fact that many players believe it to be an inevitable necessity. It takes an outsider like Marcel Marceau, the famous French mime artist, to make us aware of its absurdity. After an obviously very difficult bravura piece (on an invisible violin with an invisible bow) he walks off the stage with his left shoulder still raised high enough to touch his ear.

One of the most important factors in the gypsy's power of communication is his 'rhythmic pulse'; an organic pulse, which involves his whole body, not only his arms and hands. As rigidity is one of the basic causes of stage fright, this total interplay of motion and balance is as necessary to its elimination as blood is to the circulation. So, even if we do not get anything else from the gypsies, we *could* derive from them their total interplay of motion and balance, through their rhythmic pulse.

This is what differentiated Kreisler from all other players in his time—what made audiences stand up all over the world when he appeared on the stage—his ability to combine the ease of a gypsy with the music of Bach.

The gypsy violinists are as full of this free life-giving movement as jazz players and pop musicians are in *their* field of music. It is as obvious to the eye as it is to the ear that the music comes from the entire beings of these players. They use their particular instruments, be it violin, saxophone, guitar or what have you, only to *transmit* their musical imagination and physical energy.

However, in order to understand the nature of the organic rhythmic pulse, it is important to differentiate between *natural* and *unnatural* movements. Any movement which depends on, or is the cause of, the flexibility of the joints (such as the shoulder sockets, elbows and wrists) is natural, while movements which are merely compensatory for stiff joints in the arms and legs are unnatural. For example, the bending of the knees is natural because it happens constantly and organically in our every-day life, without us even being aware of it. On the other hand the typical violinist movement of twisting the torso left and right is unnatural. The *desire* to move while playing the violin, is very great in us all. So the twisting of the torso left and right often becomes a compensatory movement for stiff arms and rigid knees. In fact, the degree of twisting the torso, or tapping with the foot, often is in exact correspondence with the stiffness in the arm and leg joints.

It is also important to realize the significance of movement as such, apart from violin playing. Movement is life itself. If we come to think of it, we are in movement all the time, even when we sleep. When we stop moving we are dead. The power of movement is incalculable. Compare, for example, the magnitude of Mount Everest with that of the sea. How awe-inspiring, enormous and terrifying Mount Everest seems to the beholder. Yet if one asked which had more power, the mountain or the sea, the answer, of course, would be the sea. Why? Because the sea could wash away and obliterate Mount Everest by its sheer power of movement.

Furthermore, it is important not to confuse the concept of relaxation with movement. The word 'relax' is often used but not often enough understood. According to the *Pocket Oxford Dictionary* its definition is: 'cause or allow to become loose or slack or limp. Enfeeble, enervate . . .'. Among the examples it gives is a 'relaxed throat' which is described as a form of 'sore throat'.

As violin playing consists mostly of purposeful, vigorous and strong actions, the desire to relax while realizing these actions can create serious conflict in one's nervous system, because of trying to combine two actions which cannot be combined—such as being vigorous and enervated at the same time. It is essential that the significance of the natural, organic movements, with their inherent powers, are understood correctly and applied systematically.

The principles of the Fundamental Balances in violin playing, set down in *A New Approach to Violin Playing* and *The Twelve Lesson*

15

Course, remain the same, and so constant reference to them with a certain amount of repetition will be inevitable. However, in order to eliminate stage fright by a systematic procedure, it will be necessary to explore further aspects of them and then to combine these aspects with an active and constructive thought process.

The mind and the body are so closely connected that complete release from tension and anxiety in violin playing can be achieved only through the combination of a certain mental attitude, with an active physical balance.

As was said before, the causes for stage fright seem to fall into three categories: (1) physical; (2) mental; (3) social. Although they appear in this order, they interlink and are equally deep-rooted. The first step is to clarify the causes of each aspect of anxiety within its own entity. The second step is to find the appropriate cures with the relevant exercises for each cause. The third and last step is to inter-relate all three of the causes and cures. Once this is achieved, stage fright will give way to a feeling of freedom and confidence. It does not happen from one day to another. It is a training just like any other training. The difference is that it applies to *all* players and becomes a constant development instead of one single achievement.

III

The Physical Aspects of Stage Fright

1. The fear of dropping the violin

2. The fear of the trembling bowing arm

3. The fear of being out of tune

4. The fear of high positions and shifts

In order to understand the causes of the physical aspects of stage fright, and to assimilate the cures, it is important that this part of the book is not read at one sitting. For best results, it is advisable to take each part out separately with the appropriate exercises suggested within it. And only when all parts are clear by themselves should they be combined into one co-ordinated whole.

1. *The fear of dropping the violin*

CAUSES
1. Rigid stance with the feeling of an abyss underneath the instrument.
2. Excessive head pressure on the chin-rest.
3. Excessive inward twist of the left arm.

CURES
1. The stance with motion and balance through the application of the rhythmic pulse, and singing.
2. The differentiation between live weight and dead weight.
3. The elimination of the 'violin-hold'.

The fear of dropping the violin is so universal among violinists that there are references to it even in the most unexpected places. For example the programme notes of one of Daniel Barenboim's concerts say that his career began as a violinist at the age of three, but when, at the age of four, he discovered that the piano had three legs which supported it, he immediately switched over, and never looked back since.

Most of us know from everyday experience that when we are anxious about something there is a feeling of tension throughout the body. Now, for many players, the very thought of having to hold the violin is enough to create rigidity all over his body, including his knees. And the old saying 'he steeled himself' seems to apply more to playing the violin than to any other activity. Especially as the violin-hold is closely connected with the stance. In fact it is one and the same thing.

So the first step towards the release of all possible tension, is to establish a self-generating motion and balance (in the form of an organic rhythmic pulse) in the stance itself without even thinking of the violin.

It is important to understand that the organic rhythmic pulse, with its power of communication, is the very essence of music, and it must generate from the body itself. But it is also important to understand that for us violinists (because of the tensions connected with the hold), the rhythmic pulse will not happen by just wishing for it. We have to learn to apply it before it becomes a self-generating process.

EXERCISES (1)

The first exercise is to establish the stance, without the violin, based on the principles of the Fundamental Balances described on page 5 of *A New Approach To Violin Playing*. Then settle into a continuous rhythmic pulse which goes through the *whole* body. This is a very simple exercise. Count aloud up to, let us say, four. Accompany the counts with down and up *knee bends* and with *clapping of the hands*. Imagine that the body is made of coils of spring (like a well sprung sofa) which rides on the elasticity of the knee bends. The count can vary of course to any rhythmic beat desired. Then take any given piece of music and go through it with the rhythmic pulse, phrase by phrase, involving the *whole* body. If at first this exercise feels foolish or awkward, especially the knee movements and the counting aloud, get the metronome going as well, but *not instead* of doing it yourself.

The second exercise is to *sing* the pieces phrase by phrase, accompanied by the previous exercise of the rhythmic pulse.

Few violinists realize that singing (with the rhythmic pulse), away from their instruments, is one of the greatest releases from tension and anxiety in violin playing, apart from being the *real* inner source of their musical impulses. For, how can one possibly communicate if the music itself (the *tune* with its rhythmic pulse) is not established in the very soul of one's being? In order to achieve this, the aural image must be allowed to develop freely, without the impediments of an instrument. Our artistic potential can be realized only if we learn to become musicians first and violinists second. Singing is as old as the hills, the most ancient form of musical expression, and its curative value in the release from tension and anxiety in violin playing can not be emphasized enough.

19

Sing

The important thing is to learn—in our strong, weak, beautiful or ugly voices—some tunes, and to feel their spiritual content; while independent of any instrument, they permeate us and others through us. Only after this shall we be able to play an instrument in such a way as to produce genuine music and not mere sound.*

The next important procedure is to eliminate the very idea of 'violin-hold'. The prevailing attitude that the violin is held by the chin dropped vertically on the chin-rest is the cause of most of the problems. This does not only localize the hold in one spot (between the chin and the shoulder) but the harder the chin presses downwards on the chin-rest, the harder the shoulder has to counter-press underneath. This is a law of nature. Any downward vertical pressure requires the same amount of counter-pressure from underneath. So fatigue, often accompanied by acute pain in the left shoulder, is a well known violinistic malady. To a great many players the part of the violin which juts away from the body, appears to be a dead weight which hangs over a precipice. And of course, the fear that this precious possession may fall into such emptiness underneath exaggerates the necessity of pressing the chin into the chin-rest.

This is especially apparent when one asks a violinist to play a passage (or even only a few notes) with his head completely off the violin. To many players this seems an impossible task at first because of the anxiety of 'what will then hold the violin?' I gather that the prevailing attitude is not only that the chin must press downward on the violin as hard as possible (in spite of the virulent red patches on the chin) but that the violin must also be held *upward*. But when I see a violinist with the violin held high and the body stiff and rigid with anxiety, I cannot help but think of Jancsi, the hedgehog my children used to have, holding *his* quills rigid when *he* smelled danger. Hardly a position to enhance one's desire to give pleasure to others.

Therefore, this is the moment, when dealing with the violin-hold, that the active and constructive thought process should become just as important as the application of the Fundamental Balances; such as the differentiation between live weight and dead weight.

For example, think of the difference between carrying a child who is awake in one's arms, or carrying the same child when he is asleep.

*Helga Szabo on *The Kodaly Concept of Music Education*, Boosey and Hawkes, London, 1969.

20

The one awake can be carried quite a distance with relative ease compared with the child who is asleep and hangs as a dead weight in one's arms. Yet the weight of the child remains the same regardless of whether he is asleep or awake. The difference between dead weight (which is motionless) and mobile weight (which by its perpetual motion is alive) is tremendous. It is extremely important to understand the full significance of this difference (motionless= dead, mobile=alive) in relation to the violin-hold.

The whole magic and mystery of the violin as an instrument is based on the fact that *it is alive*. According to a Hungarian story (perhaps because the violin is considered such a difficult instrument) it is the creation of the devil itself; and as, to my knowledge, nobody has come up with a more convincing origin so far, this is as good a story as any. The fact remains that it is a unique instrument with unique communicative powers. So, in order to do it full justice (both physical and mental), we must learn to think about it and handle it as if it had a life of its own which, as most of us know, it has. But to infuse it with our own 'aliveness' we must be able to envelop it with our own organic movements.

This is only possible if we can learn to make our arms feel as light as feathers and as full of motion and balance as the wings of a bird.

The difference between lifting and suspending the arms and the see-saw image is described in *The Twelve Lesson Course* with appropriate exercises (pp. 3, 4). Here I would enlarge on the differences with a further example, because its execution tends to increase the weightless, wing-like sensation in the arms.

If one lifts one's arms from a natural, downward-hanging position to mid-air, into the playing position, one tends to carry out this movement from the hands, that is the hands *tend* to lift the arms. The trouble is that the weight of the arms is too much for the hands and rigidity sets in almost immediately. And as this mid-air position (especially if it has to be held for any length of time) is contrary to their natural activities, the arms soon begin to feel heavy, full of fatigue, and one is longing to drop them back to their original downward-hanging position.

But if you lift your arms *above* your head first and then *drop* them lightly downward (with your elbow bent) into the position of violin playing, the movement is controlled by the upper-arms, which by

21

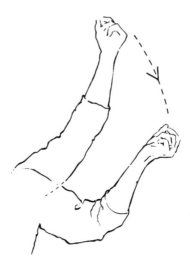

their very control create a suspended, marvellously weightless feeling throughout the arms and hands (fig. 1).

It also helps to imagine that the arms themselves are borne on currents of ever-moving air which by their perpetual motion create a feeling of active 'aliveness' in them.

This organic motion and balance in the arms is ready then to envelop the violin and transmit the natural energy of the body to it and *through* it.

In order to eliminate both the 'feeling' and the 'thought' that the violin is held, the following exercises, in addition to those already described in *The Twelve Lesson Course* (pp. 3, 4, 5), are very useful.

EXERCISES

Place the violin on the piano or on something equivalent in height, with the scroll pointing to your left. Then stand parallel to the instrument with your right arm nearest to it. Establish the spring elastic stance. Lift your left arm above your head, then drop it into the suspended position as if playing the violin. Make certain that the arm, especially the upper arm, is as light as a feather. And in order to avoid rigidity there should be a continuous sideways swing in the arm socket, so that the upper arm swings slightly to the *left*, away from the body.

22

(Both in *A New Approach To Violin Playing* and *The Twelve Lesson Course* I advocate a straight wrist in order to avoid an exaggerated backward or forward bend. But through experience I have learned that the best way to achieve continuous motion and balance is to forget the image of the violin-hold altogether and let the hand fall into the *natural* place from the suspended arm position. If there is no tension in the wrist, the hand will fall slightly backwards, away from the body, which curiously enough resembles a graceful 'giving' gesture, sometimes associated with those delicate little Oriental statuettes one sees in antique shops or museums.)

Make certain that the head too is in a perfectly natural position, neither lifted nor dropped. It should be in the same position as when talking to someone who is of equal height.

Maintaining the left arm and wrist position as described, lift the violin by placing your right hand on the right side of its body, with the thumb on the belly and the fingers on the back (fig. 2). Then (with the idea that the violin is just as light as your arm) insert it into this ready-made, air-borne position. Make certain that the violin *rests* on the collar bone and that it is *not* tilted upwards! And that the chin is so light on the chin-rest that it exerts no pressure at all. At the same time ensure that the neck of the instrument rests *lightly* in the space between the thumb and index finger while the hand is in the giving position. The latter is a most important point if we want to play through the violin and not on it. For releasing a rigid thumb position see pp. 43-46.

The idea that both the arm and the violin are light and suspended is enhanced by the thought that the chin-rest and the neck feel soft

Fig. 2

23

to the touch too, as if they were made of silk and satin. It is important to realize that our sensory responses do vary according to the texture we handle. Touching something made of fur and velvet creates quite a different sensation in us from touching something coarse like rock or rope.

> Our violin teaching does not use enough of the opportunities residing in our improvement of tactile faculties, it fails to approach violin performance from this aspect . . .*

However, if a player is so used to gripping the violin (which is most often the case) that he finds it impossible to imagine, and therefore to experience, this light feeling of arm, violin and head, and even more impossible to accept the concept that there should be, in fact, *no* violin-hold at all, an additional exercise is recommended. This consists of transferring the responsibility of holding the violin (from the pressure of the chin) to a different place altogether.

First of all feel with your hand how the crown of your head curves forward. Then *imagine that this curve links directly into the curve of the chin-rest.* Establish well in your mind this link between the curve of the crown and the curve of the chin-rest. Then tilt the crown slightly backwards so that the weight of the head is entirely on the back of the head. At the same time try to stroke the chin-rest with your chin very lightly and gently from side to side as if it were something soft, tender and alive. Spread the chin all over the chin-rest so it fills the whole space, the same way in which a fat person overflows a chair. The backward link of the head will provide a firm hold in spite of the light stroking action of the chin. It will also eliminate the necessity of the downward pressure of the chin with the corresponding counter-pressure of the shoulder underneath. And as this tenacious and anxiety-making grip dissolves, the player is well on the road to movement and to no violin-hold.

With some players (whose neurosis about the hold is so advanced that they cannot accept the weightless feeling of the violin, however hard they try) it is necessary to make them shed *all* responsibility concerning the hold Instead, they are asked to close their eyes while *I* insert the violin into the weightless nest of their arm and head.

The Physiology of Violin Playing, by Otto Szende and Mihaly Nemessuri, Collett's Ltd., London, 1971.

24

They are assured that I will keep on holding the instrument while their eyes are closed, so they don't need to feel the weight at all. Then they are to tell me if they feel it when I take my hand away.

If they open their eyes too soon and *see* me take my hand away the violin becomes heavy again. But if their eyes remain closed long enough for me to carry out this experiment, they can never tell the difference. And when at my request they do open their eyes and see that the weightless feeling is possible even without my support, the surprise they experience allows a curative process to begin. This kind of work is especially useful at Lecture Demonstrations, or in any kind of group work.

There should be no limit to the imagination and exercises concerning the *lightness* of the left arm and head, and the weightless feeling of the violin. For example, another way to pick up the violin (in order to avoid both the thought and the feeling of picking up something heavy) is in the third position with the fingers spread all over the strings while the thumb is on the back of the violin pointing towards the end-pin. Then put the violin on your collar-bone and see how wonderfully light it feels. This idea, by the way, originates with Heifetz.

Once this suspended light feeling is established there are three further exercises which help assure the *freedom* and *mobility* of the left shoulder-socket.

(1). Put the violin on the collar-bone according to one of the previous suggestions. Then lift both arms above your head with the elbows slightly bent and rest the hands on the crown (fig. 3). Bend your knees, open your mouth wide and say "AAAAH". If you are

Fig. 3

25

frightened of dropping the violin while lifting the arms, do this exercise over a bed or sofa, to be assured of having something soft underneath and to eliminate any possible anxiety of the violin being hurt were it to fall. But of course it does not fall. In fact once you eliminate the original fear (hence the necessity of a bed or sofa) you will find that you feel more comfortable and mobile than you have ever felt before. In very severe cases of anxiety about the violin-hold, I actually ask the player to *drop* the instrument on something soft. The actuality of the dreaded happening is, in most cases, a great psychological release. However, as I said before, this is only necessary when the fear of dropping the violin is very severe.

(2). Put the violin on the collar-bone into playing position as before according to one or other of the suggestions. Then swing your arm underneath back and forth as if you were walking. Make certain that the left arm swings as freely as the right, especially when it swings backwards (fig. 4). Stand over something soft as before when doing these exercises.

Fig. 4

26

(3). Put the violin on the collar-bone, so it is in playing position and imagine the crown of the head 'linking' (*gently*) into the chin-rest. Bend forward from the waist with your arms hanging in front of you (fig. 5), and you will see that the violin cannot, in fact, fall, even in this position. Make sure you do this exercise over a soft bed or sofa to eliminate all possible anxiety. Because in order to eliminate the existing tensions in connection with the hold it is of paramount importance that these exercises are not looked upon as so many challenges. Instead they should serve as active proof to the conscious and subconscious fears that the violin is light, alive and is in continuous movement with our own body so that it is not at all necessary to grip or even to hold it.

The very term violin-hold can create such far-reaching tensions and anxieties in many players that it is advisable to eliminate the terminology altogether. I have found that words like rest, place, link, nestle, cradle, not only manage to replace the traditional expression of violin-hold successfully, but that they create an active and curative thought process as well.

Fig. 5

2. The fear of the trembling bowing arm

CAUSES
1. Blockage in the rhythmic pulse because of excessive bow-grip.
2. Rigid fingers and thumb because of vertical pressure on the stick.
3. Excessive wrist movement caused by a stiff elbow.
4. The straight-line idea of the down and up strokes.

CURES
1. The inside-outward rhythmic impulse with the elimination of the bow-hold as such.
2. Eliminating finger-pressure by the balance of the thumb.
3. Transferring bow-motivation of the strokes to the shoulder-socket.
4. The idea of a curved line in the bow strokes.

A major cause of that dreaded disease—stage fright—lies in the complexities of the neuromuscular activities involved in violin playing. Watching a beginner trying to cope with the instrument, one cannot help wondering if there is any other activity in the world which demands the same amount of co-ordination. And how many players have either the inclination or the time to spend their lives studying neurophysiology, kinesiology and biomechanical motor behaviour, not to mention psychic behaviour, in order to play the violin? But even if one devoted one's life to these studies, it would be very difficult to achieve total co-ordination (such as violin playing demands) from a set of rules. The nervous system consists of such miraculously intricate and exact intercommunication that there is not one action which does not trigger off myriads of instantaneous motions throughout the whole body.

The interplay of mind and body is still something of an enigma in the scientific world, but there are fascinating new discoveries all the time. For example, the chapter 'Music and Nervous System' in Terence McLaughlin's book *Music and Communication** is full of interesting information.

The only factor which can ensure a completely free co-ordination in violin playing is the over-all perfection of our human mechanism. This is where the gypsies score way ahead of us, in their acceptance

*Faber and Faber, London, 1970.

28

of and reliance on an instinctive and organic movement pattern, combined with the conception of 'let it happen'.

The reliance upon instinct, of 'let it happen', applies to us all, but only when the movements relate to ordinary, everyday activities such as walking, running, writing, typing, etc. For example we take it for granted that the movements of everyday activities are always carried out by inside-outward impulses, the source of which is right in the centre of the body itself. We would consider it very odd indeed if somebody threw a ball from his fingers, while the hand and arm followed the movement backwards, via the shoulder, to the energy source of the body. Yet we don't seem to think it odd at all when the bow is pushed and pulled by the fingers and wrist with the arm following behind.

The acceptance of the fact that the energy impulse in violin playing is manifested in the rhythmic pulse and is directed from inside-outward, is one of the most important factors towards the elimination of stage fright in general, and of the trembling bowing arm in particular. For these inside-outward rhythmic energy impulses will not only ensure the fundamental play-actions of a co-ordinated arm movement, but will also help convey the natural energies of the body, *through* the arm, hand, bow and instrument to the listener, in the form of music. In other words it will establish organic communication.

However, in order to be *able* to transmit these inside-outward energy impulses direct to the listener, it is obviously very important that there are no hold-backs or blockages in the arms and hands. These blockages are usually manifested in stiff fingers, wrist and elbow, which by their very stiffness impede the flow of the natural energies, and result in the trembling bowing arm.

The principles related to the 'Fundamental Balances' and the 'Self-propelled Play-actions of the Bow-strokes' set down in *A New Approach to Violin Playing* (pp. 22, 23, 24) and in *The Twelve Lesson Course* (pp. 6-17) remain the same. However, since the publication of these books, experience has shown me that the very idea of bow-hold (as it was with the violin-hold) is enough to create tension in the fingers. Therefore, just as there is no such expression as baby-hold, dog-hold, suitcase-hold, tray-hold, etc., it is advisable to do away with the bow-hold as well.

29

The fear of slithery, crooked strokes and the whistling or crunchy sounds are well known to us all, and the anxiety to hang on to the stick with the fingers (in a desperate effort to control the strokes) is a common phenomenon, especially obvious in the case of beginners. Hence the bow-hold, or bow-grip. Now the only way to release the anxiety in the fingers (and, with that, release their hold or grip) is to establish sufficient balance in the thumb *underneath* the stick. But as with all fundamental balances, this can be established only if the thumb is allowed to create its own natural position.

If the thumb is in its natural bent position (as when holding a pencil) the tip area will be under the stick, while the bent part (somewhere between the nail and the joint) will touch the ferule, or the hair, depending on the size of the thumb. This double contact is of major importance because the *thumb is the only digit which is in touch both with the hair and the stick*, that is, with the top and the bottom part of the bow, and thus is able to create a link with a springy self-generating balance, between the arm and the bow. But it is very important to make sure that it is the hair (or ferule) which *leans against the thumb* and *not* the thumb which is pushed against the hair (or ferule). This is because if the thumb pushes against the hair (or ferule), the muscle under the thumb will be strained and hard, but if the hair (or ferule) *leans* against the thumb, the thumb-muscle will remain soft and springy. Once the double contact of the thumb with the bow is well established, make certain that the end-pads of the four fingers are off the stick and are slightly curved at the joints under the nails, so that the fingertips are not in the position to grip the stick even if they wanted to.

EXERCISES

First, establish motion and balance throughout the whole body (see pp. 18, 19). Then put your arms above your head without the violin and bow, and drop them into playing position. It is just as important to establish a weightless feeling in the right arm as it is in the left. But while the left arm is suspended, the right arm (because of the hand facing downward) is in a floating position. The image of the violin with the bow on the string ought to be as strong and vivid a feeling as if they were actualities.

Place the violin in playing position according to one of the exercises (see pp. 23-27), then lift your right arm above your head, with the bow in your hand, and let your arm fold together at the elbow and the wrist, and with a leftward tilt (*of the arm*) alight on the 'G' string, just above the nut (approximately where the silver wrapping ends towards the middle of the bow). Feel the hair (or ferule) *lean* against the thumb and at the same time make a mental note of the fact that the string *supports* the bow and the bow *rests* on the string.

Make sure that the elbow and wrist joints *are* flexed and that the tip area of the thumb is not pressing upward against the stick. Then take your fingers slowly off the stick (fig. 6), and see and feel how the link of the thumb and the support of the string is all that one needs for balance and security. When you can lift off your fingers with ease and confidence while the bow is on the 'G' string, try it on the 'D', 'A' and 'E' strings as well. This exercise should be done only when the bow is stationary. However, if the balance in the thumb is well established, it can be carried out at any part of the bow, including the tip.

Fig. 6

During the strokes, (because of the continuously shifting weight-adjustment of the bow) the fingers are to remain on the stick in a light resting position as natural counter-balance to the thumb. But it is vitally important that the end-pads of the fingers remain off the bow with the joints under the nail slightly curved.

In many cases (in the desire to loosen the grip) there is a tendency to lift the second and third fingers off the stick during the strokes. But this results only in a compensatory pressure in the index and little fingers.

31

So the salient points during the strokes are:
1. Double contact of the thumb;
2. A light resting position of the fingers on the stick, while the end-pads of the fingers are away from the nut and are slightly bent at the joints.

(A) THE STROKES

The next step, when dealing with the strokes, is to eliminate all possible blockages in the elbow and wrist joints and to establish a self-propelled arm movement with the bow acting only as an extension to and transmitter of these movements (see *The Twelve Lesson Course* pp. 10-22 and pp. 70-73).

In order to achieve this, it is important to understand that the weight distribution and rhythmic division of the arm and bow are not only interrelated but are a combined manifestation of the inside-outward energy and rhythmic impulses. The simplest way to understand this is to realize that the length of both the arm and of the bow consist of two halves, i.e. the upper-arm and forearm and the lower and upper halves of the bow. But it is important to note, that this division, both in the arm and in the bow, is not decided by metric measurements of two halves but by the balance of their respective weights. For example, let us take the length of the bow. Now, in order to find the middle by balance, stretch your left index finger in front of you (as when pointing towards something). Place the bow on it as near to the hand as possible, with the hair facing you. Find the centre by balancing the bow on the finger. As you will see, the lower half (the one nearer to the nut) is much heavier and therefore has to be considerably shorter in length than the upper half in order to balance (fig. 7). Then flex your arm at the elbow and wrist into playing position without the bow, and note that the upper-arm is heavier and shorter than the forearm.

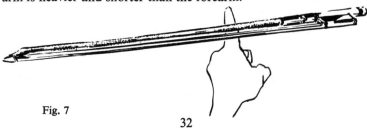

Fig. 7

32

Now, again in order to simplify, let us say that crotchets are to be played with the whole arm and whole bow, while quavers are to be played with either the upper-arm or forearm and the lower or upper half of the bow. As we usually begin with a down-stroke, at the nut, let us begin with the quaver strokes at the lower half of the bow, but at first without using the bow.

1. Drop your right arm from above your head into the weightless, suspended playing position, as if playing at the nut of the bow, with the elbow and wrist completely flexed (see illustration 12 in *The Twelve Lesson Course*). Then let your upper-arm swing out, away from the body *sideways* from the shoulder socket. If the arm is airborne and feels as if it were weightless, this motion will be completely self-propelled. Also because this swinging upper-arm is in an inside-outward natural impulse, the elbow, wrist and fingers will remain flexed and will swing with the arm movement, *without* any segmented movements of their own. In other words, the sideways swing of an airborne upper-arm will create a self-propelled, co-ordinated movement in the whole arm. It is important to note that this upper-arm movement is not an up and down action but a *sideways swing from the arm socket* (out and away from the body), and that the elbow does *not* open and shut at the lower half of the bow (fig. 8).

Fig. 8

2. Now try the same movement with the bow. You will see that if you drop your arm from *above* down on the string and allow the

33

elbow and wrist to flex into their natural curvature, *the weight of the upper-arm will act as a balance to the weight of the bow.* This balance will not only create a wonderful feeling of security in the player but it will also eliminate the necessity of tilting or slightly lifting the bow with the fingers in order to avoid a crunchy sound. Also you will see that this natural *sideways-swing* of the upper-arm will correspond with the exact length of the lower half (by balance) of the bow. The sound will be clear and rhythmical and the player will experience a feeling of over-all well-being.

So there are three salient points in the lower-half quaver-bowing:

1. The double contact of the thumb with the bow.
2. The sideways swing of the upper-arm (*without the elbow opening or the wrist pulling or pushing*) corresponds with the length (by balance) of the lower half of the bow.
3. "There is no bow" and "There is no bow-hold" is an important thought process.

The upper-half quaver-bowing begins at the middle (by balance) of the bow. And just as the lower-half quaver-bowing depended on *not* opening the elbow, this stroke depends entirely on the *opening* and *shutting* of the elbow joint.

In my experience the majority of players find it difficult indeed to flex their elbow-joints freely in the upper half of the bow, and the degree of stiffness in their elbow-joints depends entirely on the degree of their bow-grip.

For example, stretch your right arm in front of you. Then grip an imaginary object hard with your fingers. Note how stiff the elbow-joint becomes as a result. Release the finger-grip and the tension in the elbow-joint will be gone too. As the bow-grip is a very widespread habit among violinists, a great many players suffer from a chronic stiffness in their elbow-joints. It is a by-product of leading the strokes with the fingers and wrist (see p. 29), and a predominant cause for the trembling bowing-arm.

What is more, many players are so used to having a stiff elbow-joint that they are not even conscious of it. They feel that something is wrong or, in any case, not right, but they are not aware of what it is. So after a while this feeling of discomfort and anxiety is put down to the difficulties connected with violin playing or, (which is much more harmful) to their personal shortcomings. The following elbow exercises without the bow seemed to have been helpful to a great many players:

3. Drop your right arm from above your head into the position of violin playing with the wrist and elbow flexed (see illustration 12 in *The Twelve Lesson Course*). Cap the outside of the elbow-joint with your left palm and then push against the knob (figs. 9 and 10). You will see that if you push against the right spot, the arm will not only fly open, but you will not even feel the movement.

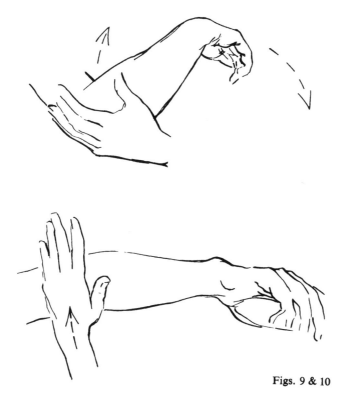

Figs. 9 & 10

Equally, while your arm is open (palm to the floor) in front of you, a downward push (with the left fingers) on the *top-outside* of the upper arm, just above the elbow-joint will allow the arm to

35

fold together (figs. 11 and 12). You will see that while the left hand manipulates the elbow, the wrist of the bowing arm will flex only as a follow through of the arm movement and not as (in so many cases) an aggressive activator. However, the majority of players are *so* used to leading from the wrist even when only imitating the strokes, that the moment the left hand stops manipulating the elbow, the wrist is apt to take the lead again.

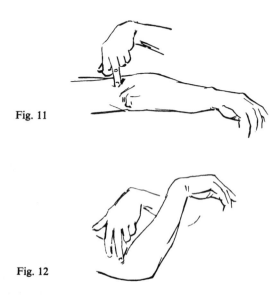

Fig. 11

Fig. 12

So, it is advisable to try the above exercise, with the help of the left hand and without the bow, every day, until the movements become self-propelled, even when connected with the bow-strokes. In other words, until you learn to 'let it happen'.

4. Then drop your arm with the bow on the open string at the middle-by-balance. Make certain that the bow *rests* on the string while the fingers *rest* on the stick. Remember to lean the ferule against the bent thumb and that there is no bow-hold. Note the *upward* curve of the stick in the upper half of the bow. Now let your arm swing open from the elbow joint *in front of you* as before, into an *upward curve*, until the bow is at the tip. Then let the arm fold back on itself in a downward curve until the bow is back at

its original point at the middle-by-balance. Make certain that the stroke *is* from the elbow-joint and *not* from a pull of the wrist and fingers.

This upward-swing of the arm (see *A New Approach To Violin Playing*, pp. 10, 11, 12), will correspond with the curve of the stick in the upper half of the bow, while the downward swing of the arm, (when coming down from the tip) will ensure a natural, inaudible bow-change.

If the elbow-joint is flexible, this springy opening and shutting of the forearm will become an autonomous action and will correspond exactly to the length of the upper half of the bow. And it will create (as did the lower-half bowing) an over-all feeling of well-being.

However, it is important to realize that the contradiction in the very terminology of the strokes such as down-stroke, up-stroke, can cause considerable subconscious conflict. To many players a down-stroke means just that: a downward pull of the bow from the fingers and wrist—and an upward push also from the fingers and wrist for the up-stroke—when in reality the curvature of the stick, in the down-stroke, is an upwards sweep towards the tip; while in the up-stroke, the curvature is a downward sweep towards the nut.

As this straight line idea of the down-stroke and up-stroke is in variance with the very constructions of the bow, (i.e. with its weight distribution and balance adjustment), naturally it creates anxiety both in the mind and in the body. In order to avoid the possible consequences (exaggerated bow-hold, stiff elbow-joint, etc.), it is essential to think of a down-stroke as basically an upward sweep, and equally to think of an up-stroke as a downward sweep.

This clarification and identification of the arm movements with the actual shape and balance of the bow will do a great deal towards the cure of a trembling bowing-arm.

The salient points in the upper-half quaver-bowing are:
1. The double contact of the thumb with the bow.
2. The upper-half strokes (between the middle-by-balance and the tip of the bow) are motivated by the opening and shutting of the fore-arm).
3. The length of the fore-arm movements (from the elbow joint) correspond to the length of the upper-half of the bow.

37

4. The upward-sweep of the down-stroke and the downward curve of the up-stroke.
5. That there is *no* bow-hold, is an important thought process.

The whole bow-strokes, crotchet, minim, dotted minim, breve, semi-breve etc. are only an amalgamation of the lower-half and upper-half strokes. But in order to avoid the trembling bowing-arm, it is essential that, whatever the count of the whole stroke may be, it fits into the weight distribution, rhythmic division, and curved shape of the bow.

For example, if the count is four for a stroke, the first two beats of the down-stroke are realized by the slight sideways swing of the upper-arm, which, (because it is a small movement) will correspond with the length of the lower half of the bow. While the third and fourth beats are realized by the *opening* of the elbow joint and fore-arm (the upward curve), which (because it is a larger movement) will correspond with the longer, upper half of the bow. The reverse is true for the up-stroke.

Once the rhythmic division and weight-adjustment of the bow and arm are amalgamated into a whole, the two balanced halves (within the whole length of the bow) will take care of all possible bowing technique as a matter of course. But in order to obtain continuous release, the rhythmic pulse must always come from the body itself and must include the knees.

The exercises given on p. 19 ought to remain part of the routine of our daily practise.

The fast bowing such as spiccato in semi- or demi-semi-quavers is discussed further on under the title 'The Fear of Not Being Fast Enough.' (see p. 80).

3. The fear of being out of tune

CAUSES
1. The lack of the sympathetic vibrations of the overtones because of over-all immobility.
2. Tension in the wrist because of excessive leftward twist of the hand.
3. Rigidity in the fingers because of vertical stopping of the notes with a superimposed vibrato oscillation.
4. The anchored thumb position because of its exertive counter-pressure against the fingers on the string.
5. Rigidity in the hand because of the stretching of the fourth finger.

CURES
1. The awareness that tone production and intonation are one and the same thing.
2. The 'giving' hand position.
3. The lateral slide of the finger action with the searching touch creating a natural, self-generating vibrato.
4. The mobile balance of the thumb.
5. The elimination of stretching with the fourth finger, with the elimination of the fourth finger action as such.
6. Ear training as part of daily practice.

This particular anxiety is closely connected with tone production and vibrato—that is, with the quality of sound we produce. In fact, it has everything to do with it. Because while the painter expresses himself through lines and colours, and the writer through word constructions, the musician does so with sound. But while the nature of painting and writing is such that the ideas and emotions can be fixed forever on canvas and paper, the nature of sound is fluid, mobile, and always momentary. Even modern machinery, like the record player or tape recorder is unable to pin sound into immobility.

We all know that a musical sound results from a combination of so many frequencies, sound waves and overtones (see *A New Approach to Violin Playing* pp. 26, 27, 28). But in order to simplify the scientific terminology and to amplify the point in hand, it is

39

enough to say here that sound has two major components—movement and air. Experiments to this effect were tried as early as the seventeenth century by Guericke, who invented the air pump. And Robert Boyle concluded later that "whether or no the air be the only, it is at least the principle of sounds".

As for movement:

> The transmission of sound-waves can be made much more intelligible if we compare it with other similar phenomena which can be followed by eye—the propagation of waves on the surface of water and the transmission of sound through the atmosphere—the similarity is very close indeed and as water waves and ripples are easily observed, their behaviour helps us a good deal in the study of sound waves.*

To realize the full significance of movement and air to sound production, we should try to imagine what would happen if we attempted to sing under water, or to say something with a hand firmly clamped on the mouth. It is very important to understand that no sound of any kind is possible without the substance of air. So the very idea that movement and air are necessary to sound ought to help us to try and exclude all possible rigidity in violin playing.

Usually, the rigidity of the left hand is much more pernicious than that of the right, because most players' idea of the left-hand finger action consists of a leftward twist of the hand with a vertical pressure from the finger tip on to the string. The very terminology—to stop the sound with the finger—suggests immobility, bereft of movement and lacking sufficient air between finger tip and string, and string and fingerboard.

> It is generally recognised that the manner of stopping has a paramount influence on tone-production. This makes the intended tone quality differ from what is actually produced. Hard and liquescent stopping, false intonation, uneven vibrato, insecure change of position, etc., are in part all due to poorly developed touching that is incapable of adaptation.†

Added to this idea of stopping the string with the finger so as to create a sound in the desired pitch, one is often advised to keep the finger down on the previous note as well (in case there will be a

*The Physics of Music, by Dr. Alexander Wood, Methuen and Co. Ltd., London, 1944.
†The Physiology of Violin Playing, by Otto Szende and Mihaly Nemessuri, Collet's, London, 1971.

40

re-occurrence of that note some time later) which makes mobility in the hand even less attainable.

It is small wonder, in this rigid anchorage, that the fingers find it impossible to react to the demands of the ear, and to adjust the note if it is out of tune. And who can guarantee to be instantly right, each time, on a long length of string, on such a sensitive instrument as the violin? But, even if the fingers do happen to 'hit' on the exact spot, the moment the finger is immobilized (by its downward pressure on the string) the note becomes false. Why? Because the rigid immobility of the finger prevents sufficient circulation of air between finger tip and string, and string and fingerboard and the sound is deprived of its two major components—movement and air —and with their absence the sympathetic vibrations of the overtones (harmonics) are missing as well.

It is not always realized that tone production and intonation are one and the same thing.

> You will notice how much richer is the sound of a note that is absolutely in tune. A note infinitesimally flat or sharp lacks that rich, luscious sound that only a note perfectly in tune will give you.*

It is a fact that, as a result of this physical inability to adjust the pitch, the ear eventually stops its corrective demands. It simply refuses to hear. And intonation becomes a major anxiety. It joins the ranks of all the other anxiety groups where the demands on the player *seem* to be beyond his capacity, when in reality, this particular anxiety (like many of the other anxieties in violin playing) is nothing more than a hitherto unreleased physical blockage.

"Am I in tune?" is an often uttered plaintive cry, even among players with a fine and well developed sense of pitch, who would have no difficulty detecting faulty intonation in others.

Many players attempt to cure the feeling of over-all rigidity by a superimposed vibrato (see *A New Approach to Violin Playing*, pp. 10, 12). But this, because of its inherent artifice, tends to make the fingers press into the string even more.

It is important to note that this particular anxiety of "Am I in tune?" becomes more acute as the technical difficulties increase.

Beauty of Tone in String Playing, by Lionel Tertis, Oxford University Press, 1938.

For example, a player may hear the pitch of his 'E' perfectly well when it is in the first position, but is quite unable to do so when the same 'E' occurs in the fifth position; not to mention other 'E's in the seventh and eighth positions. This is because finger pressure tends to increase even more in the high positions with far-reaching consequences all through the nervous system of the hand and arm, especially where the thumb is concerned (see 'The fear of high positions and shifts' p. 53).

As we have seen when dealing with the problems of 'violin-hold' (see pp. 18-27) all pressure from above requires the same degree of counterpressure from below. In this case, the vertical downward pressure of the fingers on the finger-board create instant, unavoidable, and often very severe counterpressure in the thumb underneath, or against the side of the neck (fig. 13).

Fig. 13

Ivan Galamian, in his excellent book *Principles of Violin Playing and Teaching**, points out very clearly that the contraction in the thumb is 'one of the most common and most serious of faults' and that it contributes more than most other factors to the paralytic state of the left hand.

Yet tradition is so strong that in spite of his awareness of the problems, he still believes that

> the thumb has the function of exerting pressure against the playing fingers, and it can take care of this task most efficiently if the pressure acts from below in a direction opposed to the pressing fingers.

This age-old acceptance of the ever-present and unavoidable problems concerning the left thumb, has already been mentioned when quoting one of the greatest pedagogues, Carl Flesch (see above, p. 3).

*Faber and Faber, London, 1964.

This habit of pressing the thumb inwards against the neck of the violin is so strong that, almost invariably, when I ask a player to hold an imaginary violin, his thumb becomes rigid, as if pushing against something hard, although there is nothing to push against, because he has nothing in his hand. However, as I said before, the habit of counterpressure in the thumb is so deeply ingrained, that often the player is not even aware of it. All he knows is that there is a general feeling of insecurity and anxiety which he is unable to control. This counterpressure in the thumb is exaggerated even more by the need to support the neck, and is linked with the anxiety in the violin hold.

Now it is most important to note that, according to scientific experiments, the thumb, lips and tongue occupy long segments of the Rolandic cortex, (the part of the surface of the brain where motor and sensory areas are localised) and therefore are of great importance to our communicative powers.

> The thumb is the most mobile of all digits. It rests upon a unique saddle joint which enjoys great freedom of movement. In contrast the four fingers have a common carpa-metacarpal joint which permits only slight movement. The thumb is the most valued member of the hand if one can judge from the monetary worth assigned to it by workmen's compensation. Since the structure denotes function, one can hardly escape the conviction that the thumb is indeed a highly prized member of a most important segment of a greatly specialised upper extremity. It and the hand would not be so richly portrayed in the cortex of the brain if they did not play a significant role in the activities unique to man.*

Naturally, there is nobody who would not like to have a free, flexible left thumb. The point is that this desire, however strong it may be, is apt to remain unfulfilled while there is a vertical pressure from the fingers on the fingerboard. So it is of paramount importance to find a way of playing which automatically eliminates finger pressure on the fingerboard.

The best way to achieve this is to go back again to the suspended left arm and hand position, without holding the violin (see p. 22). Then place the violin (with the right hand) between the collar bone and chin while the violin neck goes *into* the space between the thumb

*'The Developmental History of the Thumb', by F. A. Hellebrandt, M.D. *The Strad*, Dec. 1969.

and index finger (fig. 14). Make certain that thumb and index finger *do not hold the neck* but that they barely touch it. The position of the thumb differs with each individual, but if it is left to itself it will find its own natural position without any trouble at all.

Fig. 14

Note that in this position the base joints are in fact below the fingerboard. As the base joints are the natural motivators of the finger action (see *A New Approach to Violin Playing*, p. 29, and *The Twelve Lesson Course* pp. 27-36) they will play an important role in the elimination of the vertical finger pressure. In this featherlight 'giving' hand position, the finger action becomes a *lateral slide* (from the scroll end in the direction of the bridge) with a backward tilt (towards the scroll) of the fingers when they are on the string (figs.

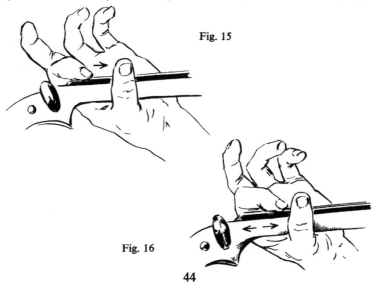

Fig. 15

Fig. 16

15 and 16). The fingertip slides on its left side. Imagine that the string is much broader than it is, and that the left side of the fingertip slides on the left side of this broad surface. Needless to say the slide of the finger is so light that it is completely inaudible. It is very important that the joint nearest the nail is well rounded, 'curled', to avoid any possible hardness and stiffness in the finger.

This sliding action and backward tilt of the fingers will not only eliminate vertical pressure on the fingerboard, but it will allow the thumb to move freely at the side of the neck, acting as a 'counter-balance' to the finger action, instead of a 'counterpressure'.

Since the publication of *A New Approach to Violin Playing* and *The Twelve Lesson Course*, experience has taught me that rigidity of the left-hand finger action was such a universal and pernicious problem that in extreme cases expressions such as 'sideways vertical action' or 'forward throw' (which I used in these books) were not enough to induce total release, even though the lightness of the action and lack of pressure were sufficiently stressed. So I have changed these expressions to a 'lateral slide' of the finger action with a 'backward tilt' of the base joints, with excellent results. The power of words on the release from anxiety will be dealt with later on in the section entitled 'The mental aspects of stage fright'.

EXERCISES
1. Put your hand in the 'violin-hold' position—without the violin. Twist your hand and wrist to the left. Press the thumb inward, toward the palm, while the fingers move up and down, as if playing on the string. Note the rigidity of the hand and fingers.

   Now let the hand drop into the 'giving' position (without the leftward twist of the wrist) and slide forward on the left side of the finger tip on an imaginary string. Note the release of tension in the thumb and hand.
2. Place the violin in playing position in the 'giving' hand. Don't use the bow yet. Slide with the first finger into the 'A' on the 'G' string and check on the flexibility of the following key points for motion and balance—thumb, wrist, shoulder socket and head.
   (a) Insert your right index finger between the root of your thumb and the neck (fig. 17). If the joint at the root gives to the touch,

45

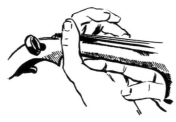
Fig. 17

the thumb is in a mobile position. If it resists the insertion of the index finger, the thumb is too rigid. This rigidity can be released by a slight inward bend of the thumb (towards the palm) *at the base joint.*

(b) Push the wrist joint gently at the back of the hand with your right index finger (fig. 18). If the wrist joint gives at the slightest touch, the finger on the strings is in a flexible, mobile position. If the wrist resists the touch, there is too much vertical finger pressure on the string. This rigidity is released by an increased backward-tilt (towards the scroll) of the first finger on the 'A'.

Fig. 18

(c) Push your left upper arm sideways (away from the body) at the shoulder socket (fig. 19). If the arm gives to the slightest touch the 'violin-hold' as such is eliminated and the thumb is released. If the arm resists the touch, there is too much pressure with the head on the chin-rest. This rigidity of the arm can be released if the exercises given for the elimination of 'violin-hold' are repeated (see pp. 22-27).

46

Fig. 19

(d) Lift your head from the chin-rest to release all possible vertical pressure (fig. 20).

Make sure that while checking on the flexibility of these key points, (thumb, wrist, arm and head), the finger does not leave 'A' on the 'G' string. Only with the finger on the string is it possible to find out whether these key points are free to fulfil their function in the perpetual interplay of motion and balance—an all important requisite for tone-production, i.e., intonation.

The same 'sliding-tilting' action and the necessity of checking on the mobility of the key points apply to the other fingers as well (see *The Twelve Lesson Course*, pp. 27-47).

Fig. 20

(A) THE FOURTH FINGER

The fourth finger needs very special attention. It seems to provide one of the greatest blockages in violin playing all over the world (see *A New Approach to Violin Playing* p. 32 and *The Twelve Lesson Course*, pp. 52-53). Since the publication of those books I have worked with players from all corners of the world whose major anxiety concerning stage fright was the fourth-finger action. In some cases, when playing in public, the finger became incapacitated to such a degree during rapid passages, double stops and trills, that the question of intonation could not even arise. And this was in spite of assiduous daily practise.

I have found over and over again that most violinists are so used to continuous stresses and strains (both in the body and in the mind) that it does not even occur to them that it could be (and indeed it should be) otherwise. This tends to apply to most players, whether they are professional or not. Most violinists are so anxious to get on, somehow or other, with the *playing* during their practise, that in spite of the increasing symptoms of tension and fatigue, they press on, quite unable to apply any curative measures. They tend to press on until an actual breakdown—a sort of short circuit in the nervous system—forces them to stop; only to go on again afterwards with the same stresses and strains as before.

The magnitude of the problem becomes apparent only when the feeling of paralysis begins to threaten each performance—in spite of the hours and hours of practise for many years. For example, quite unbeknown to most players, the fourth finger begins to get tense long before it is actually due to play. Often, quite a few notes before its turn, it begins to agitate and stretch rigidly towards its destination, affecting the whole hand (including the wrist and thumb) with the same tense rigidity. So in order to overcome this problem, in addition to the 'see-saw' image with the appropriate exercises given in *A New Approach to Violin Playing*, p. 32 and *The Twelve Lesson Course*, p. 57, subsequent exercises (both physical and mental) were developed.

The first important step was to prevent the anticipatory agitation of the fourth finger before it was used. As the player was usually not even aware of this, the only way to prevent it was to stop completely

48

while playing on the previous finger. However, easy as this idea may seem, it requires special training. For to many players complete 'stop' means a momentary bow-lift from the string with instant continuation, when in fact both the bow and the left finger should remain in a state of 'rest' on the string, while the player pretends that he has finished playing altogether *before using the fourth finger*. I have found over and over again that only this total 'stop' could put an end to its anticipatory agitation, because there is no curative value whatsoever in this 'stop' when the fourth finger is already in a stretched 'ready to do battle' position.

'Stopping' in this manner (in any given passage) is a most important and useful exercise, apart from the fourth-finger action, because it shows up (and gives the player time to notice) all the tensions and twists in the body one is not conscious of otherwise.

Try the following exercise without the bow first. Slide into the 'C' with the third finger on the 'G' string. 'Stop' completely while the 'C' remains in its place. Check with your right hand on the total flexibility of the four key points in the left arm and head. Then, instead of the fourth finger, it should be the *thumb* that slides *lightly* on the side of the neck in the direction of the 3rd position. At the same time let the wrist collapse even more to a 'giving' position, with the palm facing upward (fig. 21). (The necessity of *total* flexibility in the wrist cannot be emphasised enough).

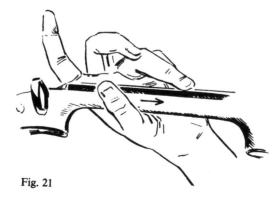

Fig. 21

49

This simultaneous forward swing of thumb and wrist will ensure a forward swing in the whole hand as well (including the base joint of the fourth finger) causing the fourth finger to slide lightly (on the left side of the finger tip) into the 'D'. Then make sure to tilt the finger slightly backwards (towards the scroll) to avoid vertical pressure (fig. 22).

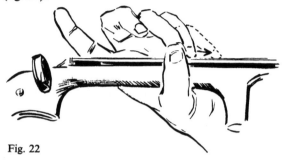

Fig. 22

Try the flexibility of the four key points with your right hand again (thumb, wrist, shoulder socket and head) while the fourth finger is on the 'D'. Then play each note twice on the 'G' string again starting from the 'A', this time with the bow, with the rhythmic pulse of two going through all these points, plus the knees. But make certain to effect a complete 'stop' before playing the 'D'.

Apply all these points to the exercises given in *A New Approach to Violin Playing*, pp. 34, 35.

As was said before, the concept (apart from the actual physical action) of sliding towards the note, then into the note, is a very important factor in the elimination of vertical pressure. For obtaining good results, it is necessary to eliminate the word 'stretch' as well. Almost invariably, the hand becomes much more supple and pliable when words like 'spread', 'fan' and 'swing' are used.

The curative measures of these exercises apply to all players alike. Even to those with very small hands, crooked, or even stunted fourth fingers. *They have far-reaching consequences not only where intonation is concerned in general, but in the release of playing double stops as well.* So far I have never worked with anybody who, under supervision, could not play thirds and octaves etc., in tune, with ease and a warm full tone with a natural vibrato, however impossible this may have seemed before.

50

The most spontaneous reaction to this feeling of ease in the fourth finger was that of a twelve-year-old boy from Canada, who was brought to me for a twelve lesson course. "Gee Whizz," he said, pacing up and down in my studio in London, looking like a miniature baseball player, with the (then) inevitable crew-cut hair. "Gee Whizz" he exclaimed each time he repeated a particularly difficult octave passage with obvious ease. "Gee Whizz". While the most imaginative and picturesque reaction was that of a violinist from Cyprus at my Summer School in Dorset. "It is like pigeons from the sleeves" he said with his inimitable English—"like pigeons from the sleeves".

Once this over-all mobility in the left arm, hand, finger and thumb is established (it must be stressed that this does not happen from one day to another and that it has to be very accurately applied, for it to work at all), it will affect all other aspects of playing as well.

1. It will allow the 'inside-outward' energy rhythmic impulses to be transmitted unimpaired all through the arm, hand and fingers.

2. It will give the player a wonderful feeling of mobility as far as intonation is concerned (because the fingers are always ready to adjust) and a feeling of technical ease encompassing double stops, trills, fast passages, etc. The unimpaired transmission of the inside-outward energy impulses also ensure a sensitive searching touch in the fingertips—which in turn ensures a natural vibrato (see *A New Approach to Violin Playing*, pp. 29-30). So intonation as such becomes a creative process—an integral part of tone production, vibrato, and musical communication in general.

> The Havas positioning of the left hand is astonishingly similar in its biological foundation, if not in detail, to the unorthodox method used by Ole Bull. This was analysed many years ago with considerable insight by anatomist Crosby, who wanted to unravel the secret of Mr. Bull's graceful pose and unique method of holding the violin. Ole Bull held the left arm with the palm facing upward, the neck of the violin reposed upon the palmar surface of the thumb. The line of support ran across the thenal eminence, that is—the thumb side of the hand designated in Havas' teaching diagrams as distinct and separate from the remainder. Crosby correctly surmised that in this position the thumb acts as a movable rest for the violin while the fingers are left absolutely free, 'for rapid and effective action on the fingerboard'. There was no grasping of the neck between the thumb and fingers and no assignment to the thumb to the duty to supply, by opposition, counter pressure for the percussive forces

of the fingers. What the thumb does also determines whether the hand, wrist, elbow and shoulder will be allowed to operate as one magnificently integrated system of levers, adjusting without strain to the demands of the music.*

This lateral slide of the fingertip and the 'giving' hand position are also very characteristic of the Hungarian gypsy violinists. For, apart from the technical freedom, it also creates a sort of 'throbbing' 'searching' sound—equipped with infinite variety, which is so typical of their unique way of communication (see the chapter on the Hungarian gypsy above).

Of course ear training should be part of our daily practice. It should be applied by all players, even by those with perfect pitch, because one's *awareness* of pitch can never be considered sensitive enough or one's reaction to the necessary adjustment quick enough. One's awareness of pitch should be looked on as a never-ending development. For example, constant checking on every 'G', 'D', 'A' and 'E' in any octave with any finger with the equivalent open string, even when perfectly in tune, will help develop a continuous heightened awareness of the search for overtones with their sympathetic vibrations.

The mental images of 'weightless arm'; 'no violin-hold'; 'a soft, silk-and-satin-textured instrument'; 'a poised hand in continuous motion and balance'; are just as necessary for the elimination of the fear of being out of tune as are the physical exercises.

*Dr. F. A. Hellebrandt, *The Strad*, 1968.

4. The fear of high positions and shifts

1. Anxiety about the violin hold.
2. Increasing finger pressure with increasing counterpressure from the thumb.
3. Rigidity in the spreadeagled hand position pressed against the rib of the violin.
4. The dearth of knowledge about the high positions.
5. Anxiety about the length of the fingerboard, because of the proximity of the eyes.

1. The realization that there is no violin hold as such.
2. Lateral slide in the finger action with raised, backward-tilted base joints. The side-to-side swinging motion of the thumb.
3. The 'silk-and-satin' conception when the hand is against the rib of the violin.
4. The awareness of the optical illusion in the length of the fingerboard, with the awareness of the anxiety produced by the focal point of the eyes.

The fear of high positions and shifts is one of the most deep-rooted anxiety factors in stage fright. It epitomises all the fears just discussed, i.e. of dropping the violin, of being out of tune, of double stops, fast passages, fourth-finger action, and so on. The fear of high positions is a compendium of them all.

The reasons for this fear are manifold. Firstly we all know (but are not perhaps consciously aware) that the higher the position, the greater is the space between the fingerboard and the string, and the greater the tendency to stop the note with increasing finger pressure. This in turn creates the necessity of a heightened counterpressure of the thumb against the neck where it joins the body of the violin, which results in an inevitably spreadeagled, rigid hand.

And this is not all. The ever-increasing pressure and counterpressure between the fingers and the thumb create the need for an equally increased pressure and counterpressure between head and shoulder (see pp. 23-27). It is like holding an orange pip between

53

thumb and index finger in a vertical position. The more one wants to 'get hold of it' by pressing it with the fingers, the more it wants to fly out. On the other hand, the lighter it rests between the touch of the fingers, the more secure it feels.

(A) HIGH POSITIONS

The trouble is that the more one tries to help oneself by 'hanging on' to the instrument in the high positions, the more insecure one feels. The fear of going *up* to a high position can be conquered up to a point, but it is quite a different matter when one has to come down from it. When going *up* to high positions, the direction is towards the main body of the violin, with the arm folding together. And the possibility of leaning against the rib of the instrument offers (to some people anyhow) a modicum of security. But the very thought of going down, or having to let go for a second (so that the hand and arm can go *away* from the main body of the violin) causes a devastating anxiety to many players. Needless to say, the greater the rigidity of the arm and hand, the greater the reluctance to let go.

We all know we should not be rigid. We would all like to have a mobile, flexible, and responsive left hand, darting up and down the violin with great ease. But we also know that, alas, the hand more often than not, refuses to oblige.

The problem begins in the third position, because this is the position where the neck joins the main body of the violin, in a downward curve underneath the fingerboard, so there is a double thickness at that point on the instrument. At the same time, the third position brings the wrist and the thumb muscle into contact with the actual body of the instrument. (I am talking of the great majority of people, of course there is always the exception.) And, as we have seen, one of the greatest incongruities in violin playing is that the much coveted, liquid sound has to be realized on an instrument which is made out of wood, and feels hard to the touch. And as our tactile senses respond by nature to the substance of any given texture, there is constant (albeit only subconscious) conflict in the player between his aural desire and the tactile realities.

In the first two positions, one has only to cope with the neck and fingerboard, and an oscillated vibrato (however unsatisfactory it may

54

be) is at least possible. But from the third position onward, when the main body of the violin is also involved with our 'touch'—the tactile sensitivity of the thumb and wrist is quick to respond to the rigid hardness of the wood it encounters. And the more true this is, the more difficult it is to attempt any vibrato—not to mention the shift.

In fact many players get so stuck against the instrument in the third position that their hands are unable to scale the seemingly formidable bastion of the rib of the violin. I have found that the germ of this problem is often present even among very fine violinists indeed, though they themselves may not be conscious of the original cause of their anxiety.

So, before going any further in dealing with the high positions, it is of paramount importance to find a way of playing in the third position first, which not only assures release from rigidity, but which prevents rigidity from the start. As we have seen, self-generating, free-flowing movement all throughout the body is the life-blood of musical communication, therefore the following exercises are based on the release of the various blockages between the hand and the violin, and on the interplay of perpetual motion and balance.

EXERCISES (1)

Put the violin into playing position, but without the bow first. Then get into the third position with the left hand.

1. Make certain that the left thumb is *not* pointing backwards towards the scroll, either at the side or under the neck, because there is a great tendency here for the thumb to try and help 'support' the violin. This tendency of course can be traced back to 'The fear of dropping the violin' (see pp. 18-19). The thumb should be just as upright, flexible and mobile as it was in the first position, acting as a counterbalance to the fingers and not as counter-pressure. The 'giving' hand position still exists, but in a slightly reduced form because the rib of the violin (underneath the neck) prevents the forward swing of the wrist and thumb, especially when playing with the fourth finger (see p. 48). However, in order to retain freedom of action, the lateral slide of the fingers (on the *left* of the fingertip) with the 'backward' and 'leftward-tilt' increase, if anything.

2. Note carefully the *exact* points where the wrist, hand and thumb muscle touch the rib of the violin *underneath* the neck. This varies a great deal with every individual. Most of us are not aware of these contacts because they are not in line with our field of vision. But wherever these contacts may happen to be, the 'touch' against the rib should consciously be softened by a slight side-to-side (from left to right) swinging motion of the hand and thumb—as if stroking something soft, like silk or satin.

   In the first and second positions, as we have seen, the base-joints are *below* the fingerboard. In the third position, however, their place varies according to the size of one's hand. In most cases the base joints are slightly above the fingerboard when playing on the 'G' string (especially when playing with the fourth finger) and below the fingerboard when playing on the 'E' string. However, it is of the greatest importance that their place is allowed to vary, and that the hand is not held rigidly in one place against the instrument.

3. Slide the first finger (on its left side) into the 'C' on the 'G' string. Tilt its base-joint backwards towards the scroll (in order to avoid vertical pressure) and at the same time tilt the side of the fingertip slightly towards the left side of the string—while continuing the swinging motion (from left to right) of the hand underneath the neck.

4. Insert your right index finger between the root of your thumb and the neck. Make certain that the joints of the thumb are flexible and that the thumb itself curves slightly inward (towards the palm).

5. Check on the thumb muscle with your right hand and make sure that it remains as soft and springy as foam rubber. At the same time make certain of the sideways swing of the left upper-arm in the shoulder socket, and of the light 'link' between head and chin rest. For that matter, constant checking of mobility in the shoulder socket and of the light link between head and chin rest is very important in all positions, but becomes increasingly so from the third position onward. Make sure that while you are checking these key points, the finger itself remains on its note, and that all the finger joints are curved, especially the one below the nail.

This 'swinging stroking' motion (underneath the neck) with the thumb and thumb muscle will ensure a poised, mobile hand in constant readiness to shift (eliminating the blockage between hand and instrument), while the lateral 'slide' and 'backward tilt' eliminates the blockage of vertical pressure and ensures a continuously free finger action and natural vibrato (see pp. 44-47).

6. Slide *into* the 'D' on the left side of the second finger (while the first finger leaves the string) and go through the same exercises. Then slide *into* the 'E' on the left side of the third fingertip and again repeat the same exercises.

7. Stop on the third finger (see p. 49). Check on the mobility of the key points, then swing the base joint of the third finger *above* the fingerboard (with the help of a left-to-right sideways swing of the thumb and thumb muscle underneath the neck), then slide into the 'F' on the left side of the fourth finger.

8. Repeat these exercises on all four strings first without and then with the bow, playing each note twice with the rhythmic pulse of two.

From the fourth position onwards the base joints should be allowed to swing higher and higher above the string and the 'lateral' sliding action of the fingers (with the backward and leftward tilt) become even more important in order to avoid downward pressure from the fingers. The necessity of movement and air (see pp. 39-41) for tone production with the natural vibrato becomes increasingly evident as the space widens between the string and fingerboard.

> The violin is of course a complicated coupled system. The bridge, the belly, the back and the contained air all take part in the vibration. Each of these has its natural frequency at which resonance may take place— the proper distribution of these natural resonant frequencies is the determining factor in the quality of violin tone.*

To many of us, the number of frequencies, velocity, sound-waves, etc., are only so many words. All we want is a liquid, expressive sound full of variety through which we can communicate. But it is important to understand that, from Mersenne, who was the first to write about the quality of sound in music in the seventeenth century

The Physics of Music, by Alexander Wood, Methuen & Co. Ltd., London, 1944.

(*Harmonis Universalle*) to Dr. Alexander Wood (*The Physics of Music*), every treatise seems to agree on the over-all importance of overtones to the quality of sound. And as the overtones depend on continuous movement and circulation of air between finger-tip and string, and string and fingerboard, a total interplay of motion throughout the hand is of the greatest importance. This is impossible to achieve through a vertical finger pressure on the string. Once this pressure is exerted (creating a chain reaction of contractions throughout the hand and arm to the violin hold itself) it is useless merely to lighten it, especially in the high position, because all one achieves is a weak sound, resembling a harmonic. No negative action or thought of 'I must not press with my fingers' will provide the necessary self-generating motions. Therefore, the importance of the 'backward-leftward tilt' of the hoisted base joints in the high positions cannot be emphasized enough. As we have seen the 'backward-tilt' creates a natural link between the fingertip and string (eliminating any possibility of vertical pressure) and provides a contact full of power, variety and motion; while the leftward-tilt of the fingertips create a sensitive, searching touch. In fact, to sustain a full, warm tone in the very high positions (such as 7th, 8th, 9th, 10th, etc.), the finger action should be entirely on the left side of the string, especially on the 'A' and 'E' strings (fig. 23).

Fig. 23

This sideways contact of the string from the seventh position onward is very important because this way the string does not even touch the fingerboard. There is a common failing for the tone to become smaller and more muffled as the positions increase in height,

58

until often, in the very high positions near the bridge, there is no tone at all. This is because the string is pressed into the fingerboard. The increased space between string and fingerboard as one gets nearer to the bridge is there for a purpose. It allows increased circulation of air which picks up the sympathetic vibrations of the overtones (harmonics) the very ingredients of a rich, warm sound. However, this sideways touch can be achieved only if the thumb and thumb muscle are supple and in continuous motion, acting as counterbalance to the finger action.

There is a point in the higher positions, when (depending on the size of the hand) the thumb muscle is completely above the belly, so that the side of the thumb itself is against the side of the fingerboard (fig. 24), (*not* against the side of the rib). This is especially helpful to people with small hands.

Fig. 24

The release of thumb and hand from pressing against the instrument gives a wonderful feeling of ease and freedom to the shifts and has a tremendous effect on the quality of tone in the high positions. But, needless to say, this can be achieved only after careful training and constant checking on the mobility of the key points, such as the shoulder socket, wrist joint, thumb, and all the joints of the fingers. The balanced head-contact with the chin-rest, with the idea of the suspended, weightless violin *without* a localized hold becomes increasingly important in the higher positions.

Think of a trapeze artist—how beautifully poised he is before taking off for a flight through the air, how his whole art depends on a continuous play-action of motion and balance in every joint of his body—then apply the same image to your left hand.

The following exercises apply to all the higher positions, starting from the fourth. They are of great importance and have helped a great many people. But they have to be applied slowly, with patience and with very great care for the *over-all* release at all the key points. Often, when one releases the thumb, the violin hold wants to stiffen —or when the arm socket is released, the fingers want to clutch, etc. So it is advisable to apply them in slow motion without using the bow at first.

EXERCISES (2)

1. Place the violin in playing position but without the bow first. Slide *into* the 'D' on the 'G' string with your first finger. Tilt the base joint of the first finger slightly backwards towards the scroll (to avoid vertical pressure) and at the same time tilt the left side of the fingertip slightly towards the left side of the string, while continuing the stroking motion of the thumb and the thumb muscle underneath the neck.

   The height of the base joint above the string depends entirely on the size of the player's hand, but if one imagines that the moment the first finger slides into the 'D' it will be followed by a fourth-finger 'D' an octave higher on the same string, both the height of the joint and the swinging attitude of the hand will be determined. Such an interval on the same string is usually quite beyond the reach of people with average or small hands and causes a great deal of stress and strain even in large hands.

   It is important to note that both the backward- and leftward-tilt vary with each player (again depending on the size of the hand). In some cases it is so slight (especially in the fourth and fifth positions) that it is not even visible, while in other cases it is an obvious physical action.

2. Make certain that each joint of the finger is curved, especially the joint below the nail, and that the pulse of two goes through the whole body including the knees, the 'head-link' with the chin-rest and the arm socket.

3. Put your right hand on the side of the violin for reassurance, then, on the first pulse, swing and curl your left thumb (underneath the neck) towards the right, so that it leaves the neck and swings right

60

above the fingerboard (on the 'E' string side), then, on the second pulse, swing it back to its original position. The finger on the string is to remain in playing position through this exercise.

4. Slide on to the 'E' with the second finger and repeat the pulsed swinging exercise of the thumb. Then slide into the 'F' with the third finger and then on to the 'G' with the fourth, repeating the same exercise.

5. Repeat the pulsed, swinging exercise of the thumb on all the strings and in all the positions, first with the right hand on the violin for assurance, and then without it. Only then try it with the bow.

6. Note the exact spot where the wrist, hand and thumb muscle touch the rib of the violin. It will be different in every position and it will vary considerably according to the size of the player's hand. Whatever the point of contact may happen to be, make certain that there is only a brushing, stroking contact during these exercises. The higher the position the more important the soft, silk-and-satin tactile image becomes. For only the use of that image will enable the thumb, in the very high positions, to find its place above the belly, next to the fingerboard—and enable the fingers to play only on the side of the string, especially on the 'A' and 'E' strings, so that the space between the string and fingerboard can remain undisturbed.

7. In the very high positions extra care should be taken to ensure that the 'head-link' with the chin-rest and the left arm socket does not stiffen during the swing of the thumb, and that the forearm just above the wrist does not lean against the violin.

It is very important that these exercises should never be allowed to become a sort of jerky, gymnastic-like challenge. They should be done, as all the other exercises have been done, only to ensure continuous motion and balance throughout the whole body. And only when the mobility of the thumb is completely ensured should the bow-stroke be applied as well.

Also, in order to eliminate stage fright, it is of paramount importance that the player is as familiar with the fingerboard in the high positions as he is with it in the first position.

I have found over and over again that even high-powered players can lose their bearing on the fingerboard above the fifth position.

Needless to say, this impedes not only the faculty of hearing but the spontaneity of the finger action as well. Hence the anxiety both in the mind and body, especially when the phrase happens to begin on a high note.

So it is highly advisable to take out, in a different position each day, the four basic exercises set down in *A New Approach to Violin Playing* (pp. 37, 38). But often, even if the player happens to know the positions perfectly, there is a tendency to test the note in the first position first and then climb up to the high note over the rib of the violin. As there is not always time for this, it is important to learn to give oneself commands for the finding of any note at random with any finger in any position.

At first start with notes which have an equivalent open string, for example a 'G' with the first finger on the 'G' string. But before anything else, make certain to register in your mind that this particular 'G' is in the seventh position. Then slide into it, from about the fourth position, with the left side of the finger on top of the string. Then test it with the open string. If by any chance the note happens to be far out, make a mental note of where the seventh position is supposed to be, and try again. Then try the same note with different fingers. Then try 'E' on the 'D' string in different positions with different fingers, the 'A' on the 'E' string, etc. When the notes with the equivalent open string are well established, try the same exercise with notes such as 'B' and 'F', etc.

This exercise is most important for the elimination of stage fright. It will help release the tension and anxiety connected with the 'no-man's-land' or 'hit-and-miss' attitude towards the high positions (provided the hand is supple and the silk-and-satin contact with the violin is well established) and thus will ensure a feeling of security and well-being while playing to an audience.

(B) SHIFTS

Once a supple hand with a free finger-action and sensitive touch is established in all the positions, to most players the shifts cease to present further problems. But to those players for whom the shifts remain a major point of anxiety, it is advisable to apply the following suggestions and exercises. They seem to have helped a great many people.

The first step is the realization that the seemingly endless length of fingerboard ("Like a veritable motorway", remarked a violist) is only an optical illusion. In reality the fingerboard is not half as long as it seems when looking down on it from playing position. So in order to register the difference between the optical illusion and reality, first place the violin into playing position, look down on the fingerboard (fig. 25), and consciously register how long it seems to be.

Fig. 25

Then follow this up by placing the instrument on the piano or on a table. Put your index fingers at both ends of the fingerboard (fig. 26).

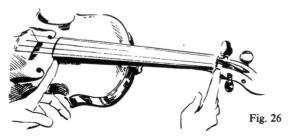

Fig. 26

Take the fingers away but keep the measured distance between them. Note how ridiculously short the distance really is. On the violin the length of the fingerboard is hardly more than the length of one octave on the piano, even on the viola it is no more than the distance between 14 notes on the piano. The sideways view and point-to-point measuring of the fingerboard seem to result in a much more effective release from anxiety concerning the shifts than if it had been measured by a tape measure.

63

However, the elongated, optical illusion of the fingerboard is only partly responsible for anxiety in the shifts. The other part is that the finger-action is also right in front of the focal point of our eyes. There is no instrument, to my knowledge, where the eye is as closely connected with the fingertip activities as it is in the violin. Consequently, (perhaps even without being consciously aware of it) the player tends to rely much more on the guidance of his eyes than on the guidance of his ears, and the shifts become a sort of vertical hopping action from finger tip to finger tip on a seemingly endless fingerboard.

In many cases this visual emphasis on the fingerboard becomes so detrimental to the aural perception that the player is quite unable to play with his eyes closed. He is so used to relying on what he sees that he is unable to rely on what he hears—let alone use the anticipatory powers of his inner ear.

This is especially evident when, after repeated requests to close his eyes, the player replies with a firm and often indignant affirmative "but my eyes *are* closed", whereas his eyes are not only wide open but, quite obvious to the beholder, are full of anxiety signals.

This type of work is especially useful at Master Classes or at Lecture Demonstrations, because it is easier for the player to believe twenty to two hundred people about his eyes being open, when he himself thought they were closed, than to believe one person, his teacher. In such cases the player is advised to tie a scarf in front of his eyes and then to try the passage again. Almost inevitably, when the ears are allowed to function unimpaired, the shifts become much more accurate and almost always there is a noticeable improvement in the over-all playing as well. But in cases where the player's anxiety about the shifts is so exaggerated that being blindfolded is not enough of a release, the following exercises are recommended in addition to those which are already set down in *A New Approach to Violin Playing* (pp. 38-40).

EXERCISES

The ascending shift

1. Play 'B' 'C' and 'C' 'B' on the 'G' string in the first position to the rhythmic pulse of two for each note, and slur two notes for a bow.

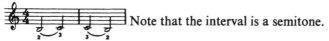 Note that the interval is a semitone.

2. Sing the 'B' 'C'—'C' 'B' to the rhythmic pulse of two.
3. Play the 'B' again but on the count of two take the first finger back towards the scroll (as if preparing to play an 'A') (fig. 27) then, on the count of three, swing it with a lateral, sliding action into the 'C' in the third position (fig. 28), and continue to play it to the rhythmic pulses of four.

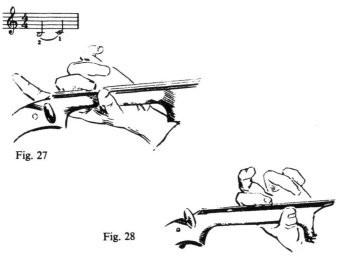

Fig. 27

Fig. 28

The descending shift

1. Repeat the 'C' with the first finger in the third position to the rhythmic pulse of two.
2. *Stop* on the 'C' with the bow resting on the string and take the second finger back (as if preparing to play a 'D').
3. Let the thumb go slightly away from the neck (*not* backwards), while the first finger releases the string as if the 'C' were a harmonic.

65

4. Swing the arm down into the first position while the second finger swings *forward* and slides into the 'B'.

The downward swing of the arm and the forward swing of the finger coincide with the continued beat of the rhythmic pulse and with the 'giving' hand position. Repeat this exercise on all strings first with the eyes open, then with the eyes closed, or, if necessary, blindfolded.

Start on the 'G' string the same exercise in the second position with the second finger on the 'C'.

(a) Play 'C' 'D'—'D' 'C' first in the same position.

(b) Sing them.

(c) Apply the shifts following the same instructions as before.

Always combine the ascending and descending shifts. Practise, as before, first with the eyes open then with the eyes closed and, if necessary, blindfolded. Repeat the same exercise in the 3rd, 4th, 5th, 6th and 7th positions as well. Then repeat the same exercises with the third and second fingers, and then with the fourth and third fingers.

Finally, combine the ascending and descending shifts into an octave run on the same string, first between the second and first fingers, then between the third and second, fourth and third. For example:

and so on.

Make sure that in the high positions the base-joints are well above the strings (with a sideways touch and backward tilt of the finger to avoid vertical pressure) and that the thumb swings above the belly in

66

the ascending shifts, and slides underneath the neck in the descending shifts. Stopping before each descending shift is highly advisable. Also, make certain that when the arm swings down into the first three positions, the hand resumes its 'giving' gesture, otherwise the finger cannot effect a self-propelled lateral forward slide into its note.

It cannot be emphasized enough that hard work alone will not be sufficient to release the anxieties in the shifts. The result of these exercises will depend entirely on a thorough knowledge of the positions and on the degree of enjoyment in the mobility and freedom throughout the *whole* body. Because it is obvious that a trapeze-artist-like hand which is constantly poised and ready to act can be achieved only through perpetual motion and balance, without the conscious (or subconscious) impediment of the violin. As was said before, the idea of a 'weightless' violin without any localized hold is more important in the shifts than almost anywhere else. In fact, the shifts, because of their dependence on mobility, can hardly ever be referred to as 'just difficult'. More often than not they are either easy or impossible. When they are made easy by this approach, the release from stage fright is incalculable. However, full benefit can be experienced only when all physical release becomes a co-ordinated whole, and is then combined with the release from the mental anxieties as well.

IV

The Mental Aspects of Stage Fright

1. The fear of not being loud enough

2. The fear of not being fast enough

3. The fear of memory lapse

4. The power of words

5. The power of imagination

1. The fear of not being loud enough

CAUSES
1. The desire for increasing loudness in the world in general.
2. The variance in the tone under different acoustical conditions.
3. The desire to hear oneself above all other instruments.
4. The impossibility of hearing one's own quality of sound.

CURES
1. The difference between hearing and listening.
2. The co-ordination of the aural and sensory reactions.
3. The development of the inner ear.

The desire to play louder and louder and the fear of not being able to do so is an increasing problem among violinists. This anxiety is due to the construction of larger and larger concert halls in order to accommodate larger and larger audiences. There is, however, a desire for an increasing loudness in the world and the noise-loving younger generation with their powerful guitars and ear-splitting discotheques do tend to affect us all, even though we may not be consciously aware of it. But while everything is becoming larger and noisier around us, the violin remains the same—delicate, sensitive, and so very fragile compared with other instruments. And as if the fear of not being loud enough were not sufficient by itself, there is also the knowledge that because of the very sensitivity of the instrument, the tone will react differently to each different acoustical condition.

Who is not familiar with the anxiety of going into a strange examination room or of going out on the platform in a darkened concert hall, not knowing what the violin will sound like? Especially in a concert hall (no matter how much one has rehearsed in it previously), one knows that the sound of the violin will be quite different again when there is an audience.

Even in everyday life, no sooner have we got used to the sound of our solitary practice in the familiarity of our room than we are immediately confronted either with piano accompaniment (which on average has five notes to every one of our own) or with being in the middle of an orchestra amongst umpteen other stringed instruments, woodwind, drums, not to mention the brass. And as one of the

70

reasons for playing the violin to begin with is usually to hear oneself play, there is an overwhelming desire to outplay the piano and, if not the whole orchestra, at least to outplay one's neighbour in the next chair!

The fear of not being loud enough tends to be at its worst when playing with orchestra accompaniment. Here it is not only a question of pitting one's tone against those of contrasting instruments, but of defending it against one's stringed brethren, sometimes fifty strong.

Not that this particular problem is unique to us: other musicians suffer the same anxieties under those conditions. "Just don't push it, honey," said Joan Sutherland, explaining to a fellow singer why her own voice always remained glossy. "Be satisfied with the size of sound you can make." But will we be satisfied? No, we won't—not with that big orchestra playing away.

The trouble is that the 'pushing it' to use her expression, not only actually diminishes the sound, but in our case it creates a whole chain of stresses and strains as well: insecurity in the violin-hold, an unsteady bowing arm, intonation, difficulty with shifts, etc., until the player is overcome with a feeling of helplessness in his efforts to be heard.

It is interesting to note that when one sees a violinist on the stage with his head tilted sideways to such a degree that his ear is practically on his instrument, he is almost always playing with orchestral accompaniment. Other players increase the movements of their bowing arm in their attempts to be heard. It is not all that unusual to see a soloist playing with such aggressive strokes that one cannot help feeling that any minute smoke may rise out of the instrument. And yet one cannot hear his tone above the orchestra.

Curiously enough these overworked, aggressive strokes are often more characteristic of violinists with a highly developed artistic sensitivity than of those with lesser talent and ability. More often than not, the desire of these players to be heard is so overwhelming that they are compelled to be aggressive from sheer anxiety. But as the motivation of these aggressive right-arm movements is usually from their wrist and fingers (and not from the shoulder socket as nature intended), they cannot convey the power of the inside-outward energy impulses (see p. 29), so the tone remains small and a loss of confidence is bound to set in with all its consequences. Even when

71

the player is fully aware of what a powerful tone he can achieve with motion and balance, the fear of not being loud enough can be so strong that he too succumbs to the stresses and strains of forcing the sound with the bow in an attempt to play louder.

Few players in my experience realize that we cannot in fact hear ourselves as others hear us. We can hear the pitch and we can hear the sound, but we cannot hear what we sound like. That would be a physical impossibility. "We can't *really* tell whether we are doing everything right, because we can't really hear ourselves," says the singer Marilyn Horne. We all know this subconsciously, and sometimes consciously, but we are reluctant to accept the fact because we are afraid that if we cannot hear ourselves, then maybe nobody else can hear us either. Acceptance comes more easily if we realize that it is the same when we are talking; we can hear what we say, but only other people can hear what we sound like. The truth of this matter becomes apparent only when we listen to a tape-recording of ourselves. It is something of a jolt (especially the first time) to hear a voice which seems to belong to a stranger, often quite alien to our image of ourselves. I, for example, cannot hear my foreign accent when I speak in English, and will never forget how shocked I was when I first heard it on the tape. It sounded like Mata Hari.

Another important point is that if there is any rigidity in the body whatsoever, the true value of what we *can* hear is gone by the time we hear it because, as we know only too well, rigidity also prevents spontaneous reaction in our sensory perception. As was said before, the nature of sound is fluid, mobile, and always momentary. It is like time. One cannot hold it back for inspection, not even for a fraction of a second.

It is the effort of listening to something that we cannot hear and which (more often than not) has already happened, that creates such seemingly unreasonable and devastating anxiety in so many players. Add to this the conscious or subconscious knowledge that the sound will depend on the acoustical conditions, and you will have the sum total of one of the most virulent and most common causes of stage fright.

The most effective cure for this particularly serious anxiety is to realize that hearing and listening are both necessary but one must learn to differentiate between them. *Often we are so busy listening*

72

for the quality of sound, which it is impossible for us to hear, that we are unable to pay sufficient attention to the pitch, which we can hear.

(A) HEARING

What is it really all about? To repeat, the acuteness and immediacy of our pitch depends on the mobility and sensitivity of our touch, which, as we have seen, is only possible if there is over-all motion and balance throughout the whole body (see pp. 18-19).

If there are no physical blockages to stop the flow of our inside-outward musical impulses and if ear training is part of our daily practice, then the demand for overtones in every note becomes a co-ordinated aural and physical reaction—without any time lapse between the hearing and the doing.

I have seen players, who thought themselves tone deaf, adjust their pitch instinctively when their physical blockages were released. And as a result, the quality of their tone improved beyond recognition, because as we have seen, intonation and tone production (containing a natural, self-generating vibrato) are one and the same thing (see p. 51). *Therefore, our interpretation of hearing should always refer to pitch.*

EXERCISES

In order to obtain the best results, the exercises for ear training should be kept as simple as possible and should always be combined with singing. They should not be looked upon as a test for perfect pitch, but as a reassurance of one's ability to respond instantly to the demands of the ear. As a matter of fact, for a continuous musical development, the daily practise of ear training should be as important for players with perfect pitch as it is for players who think themselves tone deaf. The use of a piano for these exercises is a great help. If no piano is available to create reassurance use the violin instead. In the following example I will use a piano.

1. Play the middle 'C' on the piano. Sing the 'D' a tone above it. Then play it on the piano. Play 'C' again, sing the 'E' a third above. Then play it on the piano. Then play the 'C' again and sing the 'F' a fourth above. Continue this exercise until you reach the octave. Then play the 'C' an octave above middle 'C' and sing

73

the 'B' a semitone below it, and then play it on the piano. Then play the 'C' again and sing the 'A' a third below it and play it on the piano. Play the 'C' again and sing the 'G' a fourth below it and then play it on the piano. Continue this exercise until you reach the middle 'C' again. It is very important to name the notes as you sing them.

2. Play the middle 'C' on the piano and sing a major third above it and then play it on the piano. Play the middle 'C' again and this time sing a *minor* third above, then play it on the piano. If you don't happen to be singing in tune it is most important not to get annoyed with yourself. Instead, sing it while playing it on the piano and then try to sing it alone. Play a perfect fifth on the piano then sing it, then play it on the piano again. Play a diminished fifth, sing it, play it again. Play a major seventh, sing it, play it again. If you are not correct, repeat it as often as necessary.

Practise these exercises every day as a matter of routine and correct yourself, if you are inaccurate, with the help of the piano or the violin. Think in intervals and always sing the notes with their names.

3. Play only those notes on the violin that have an equivalent open string. First play them only in the first position, i.e. the third finger 'G' on the 'D' string, the third finger 'D' on the 'A' string, the third finger 'A' on the 'E' string. Check each one of these notes with the open string. Then play each note alone. If they contain the overtones of their equivalent open string they are really in tune, and will have a lovely, shiny sound. Play these notes to the rhythmic pulse of four, slowly and quietly. *Give yourself plenty of time to hear.* Play the 'D' with the fourth finger on the 'G' string and try it out with the open 'D'. Then play and check on the fourth finger 'A' and 'E' the same way. Combine these exercises with the exercises given for the left-finger action (pp. 49-50).

4. Play all the notes with their equivalent open string in all the positions. Combine these exercises with those given for high positions and shifts (pp. 55-59, 60-61, 65-67), until the awareness and sensitivity of both your hearing and your touch become a single-co-ordinated and subconscious reaction to the desire for perfect pitch.

5. Repeat the singing and pulsing exercises on pp. 19, 84, but whatever phrase you happen to take out for this particular exercise, play it on the piano (or violin) first. If the intervals reach beyond the range of your voice, learn to adjust them within one octave. Make certain to give the notes their names while singing (see p. 81-85) with their appropriate sharps and flats first and then, because it is rather cumbersome to say F♯, B♭, G♯, etc., abbreviate them into their ordinary names, but with an inner knowledge of the accidentals. As the 'sol-fa' does not seem to be common practice either in Britain or the United States, this method of verbal abbreviation but with full mental knowledge of the accidentals, has proved to be the most helpful way of dealing with the problem. The salient points of hearing are:
1. Daily ear training;
2. The elimination of all physical blockages;
3. Instant co-ordination of the aural and sensory reactions;
4. The knowledge that intonation and tone production (containing a natural self-generating vibrato) are one and the same thing.

(B) LISTENING

But what about the 'listening' part? For, even when the co-ordination of hearing and feeling the notes is well established, we still don't know what we *really* sound like—not to other people, anyhow. Therefore, the problem of trying to listen to ourselves may persist, even after the 'hearing and reacting to the pitch' part of the playing has been successfully dealt with. One thing is certain. The 'I must not listen to myself' mental attitude will be of no help at all. As was said before, it is never any use telling ourselves what not to do. Only positive actions and thoughts will have the power to eliminate any particular anxiety. This applies to listening as well. Of course we must listen—and listen with all our might. But in order to do this properly, there comes the more important, more necessary, and most basic requirement of all musicians, especially violinists—the development of the inner ear.

We are often so busy trying to overcome the difficulties of playing the instruments that we don't even realize that the inner ear exists. Everybody who is not deaf can hear, but it takes a musician to use the inner ear. It is the same with seeing. Everybody who is not blind can see, but it takes an artist to perceive the meaning of lines, shapes and colours in the most ordinary objects around him.

Only the inner ear can link the player to the depth and inner core of the music. The sensitivity of the inner ear, like the physical aspects of playing, depends on a regular, systematic training. It goes together with the co-ordinated aural and physical reaction to the pitch. But while the overtones in the pitch provide a shiny warm sound, the inner ear supplies the sound with a meaning and colour of infinite variety. However, in order to get the inner ear to function properly, it is important that its training is quite separate from playing the violin.

The inner ear is closely linked with our imagination. In fact it is the imagination transformed and channeled into music. It is the sum total of a heightened awareness and sensitivity of all the passions, joys and sorrows in human nature.

The training of the inner ear is really a training of our imagination, which can be achieved only if it is constantly provided with information. The supply of information is not linked to music alone. No, not at all. It can be found in reading, going to the theatre, or to a football game—by watching television, children at play, sitting by the sea, or visiting a cathedral. It is really a constant process of learning to notice and absorb like a sponge the aliveness of the world around us. The imagination seems to thrive when a musician happens to be interested in painting, sculpture and architecture, not to mention literature. The emotional gains from these experiences cannot but enrich his own art—music.

A fertile imagination will not only help to make any given composition come alive, but will make the composer live as well. For who can really understand Sibelius if he has not experienced the coldness of frozen snow and ice (through whatever media). Who can really play Handel without understanding the elegance and lustiness of his century? While to play Bartok, one must have insight into what black earth under the parching sun or the death of a cow mean to a peasant. For that matter, how can one play any work without being familiar with most, if not all, of the composer's other works as well? For in no other way can the inner ear conjure up the texture of the sound best suited to a particular composition. The necessity for absolute clarity of articulation of the unaccompanied Bach can only be fully appreciated if one is also familiar with his keyboard music.

Or one must be familiar with Schubert's songs in order to produce the smooth, honey-textured sound when playing one of his string quartets.

This is where listening comes in. The listening of the inner ear. And the most important point of this kind of listening is that it is always done a step ahead of the actual playing. It is always anticipatory. The inner ear has no time to listen to the player, and no desire to do so. It is far too busy conjuring up and transposing all the information it has absorbed into active imagination of the music in hand. So by its very nature of creativity it is always ahead, compelling the player to pursue it. And so the anxiety of not being able to hear oneself and the fear of not being loud enough become non-existent. What is more, once the power of the inner ear has been discovered, its increasing perception and creativity become a never-ending development. The more the player learns to summon the imagination of the inner ear, the more he is able to forget about the extraneous part of his playing, such as his technique, his tone, the impression he makes on his listener, etc., until eventually he can forget about himself. And that is when real communication begins. For with the elimination of the self he is able to reach the very core of the music and through the interplay of co-ordinated balances is free to transmit it to the audience.

The goal is to eliminate the self—because "left to itself, the physiological intelligence is almost incapable of making a mistake".*

But needless to say, this state of bliss is only possible if a free-flowing channel of total motion and balance has been established. If there is the slightest physical blockage caused by rigidity in any given part of the body (i.e. localized violin hold, bow-grip, stiff elbow joint, etc.), the imagination of the inner ear immediately stops functioning. For just as in everyday life our limbs translate our thoughts into actions, so in violin playing the inside-outward rhythmic energy impulses become transmitters of the musical imagination.

*A. Huxley, Foreword to *New Pathways To Piano Technique*, by Luigi Bonpensiere, The Philosophical Library, New York, 1953.

1. Sit down with the music you are about to study. Make certain that before anything else, you observe the four basic directions that the composer wants you to be aware of: the key, the tempo, the dynamics, and the rhythmic pulse.

   Then, see where the first phrase ends. Then learn to note every little detail within that phrase. Does it have one culmination or several? Is the musical idea displayed in sequences? What *kind* of idea is that phrase? Festive? Delicate? Restive? Nostalgic? Humorous? (Or whatever it may happen to be.) How does it relate to its accompaniment? Has the piano—or orchestra—introduced this particular musical idea already? Or, does the solo violin part have the privilege of bringing it in first? If it has been introduced before, how was it done? In the case of orchestra accompaniment what sort of texture does the composer indicate with his orchestration? Is it a preparation for the solo part? Or is the solo part to appear as a continuation or an elaboration of the idea? And so on and so on. What other instrument could indicate the character of that first phrase besides the violin? The flute? The cello? The trombone? If it were a singer, what sort of voice would that singer need to have to sing that phrase? Tenor? Alto? Soprano? Bass?

   Imagine your favourite violinist playing that phrase. What would he sound like? What kind of tone would he use during that phrase?

2. Go through the phrase with the rhythmic pulse which involves your whole body including the bending of your knees and the clapping of your hands (see p. 19).

3. Sing the phrase first with the piano and then without. Combine it with the rhythmic beat.

4. Then play it on the violin.

   If you go over each phrase with the same awareness, you will not only achieve a hitherto unexperienced physical ease, but will enhance your imaginative powers as well. And if you continue to work like this as a matter of course day in and day out, the power of your imagination will be so intensified that you will only need to look at a piece of music for it to become instantly alive and full

78

of interest. The sign *forte*, or *piano*, will not only represent a loud or soft sound but will acquire an infinite variety of texture and colour depending on the meaning we understand in the music.

Another important point is to become aware of the different textures of sounds of the four strings on the violin. Think of the strings as if they were four voices, the 'G' string as a bass, the 'D' string as a tenor, the 'A' string as an alto and the 'E' string as a soprano.

It is very helpful to conjure up the sound of a favourite singer whose range belongs to the string we play on. Anybody who has heard a recording of Chaliapin and can re-enact the fathomless depth and variety of that voice when playing something like Paganini's *Moses Fantasia* on the 'G' string, will be amazed at what that string on the violin is capable of; or for that matter Callas (at her best) on the 'E' string; or Marian Anderson when playing on the 'D' and 'A' strings.

5. Practise the scales, playing each note to the pulse of four and conjure up the tone you associate with any given composer. Let us say the scale in question is D major. Play the scale and imagine the texture of tone to be that of Mozart. Play it again and this time adjust the tone to suit Tchaikovsky, and then again as if playing Dvorak, etc.

6. The awareness of the interval progression is another and equally important practice for the development of the inner ear. For, just as an author conveys his meaning through the use of words, so a composer communicates his meaning through the use of intervals. In fact, the only way he can express himself is through a choice of interval progressions set within a rhythmic pulse. So it is very important to learn to be aware of the meaning of intervals while practising arpeggios in the scales.

For example, to exaggerate the intensity of a dominant seventh run, give full importance to the opening major third and to the finishing diminished seventh. Or, when practising a run in the diminished seventh, make sure that you highlight the quality of the minor third progression. For that matter one ought to be constantly aware of what a world of difference there is between a major third and minor third, not to mention the drama of an augmented second, which stands for something quite different

79

from a minor third. Being in tune with a perfect pitch is quite a different thing from giving meaning to the intervals.

Now of course there are a great many violinists who are fully aware that there is much more to violin playing than moving the fingers and the bow, and to many of them the above suggestions will present nothing new. But alas, many players, even when they are aware of the importance concerning the imagination, are reluctant to give it time in their daily practice. The fear that every moment spent away from the violin will prove to be wasted, and the neurosis of compulsive playing in order to get better, are too strong. Those players who manage to overcome the 'compulsion to practise' only on the violin invariably achieve greater ease in their playing.

The salient points of listening are:
1. That while the hearing of the physical ear is momentary, the listening of the inner ear is always anticipatory.
2. The need to supply constant information to the imagination.
3. The awareness of the variety in the texture of the sound.
4. Awareness of the dramatic powers of the intervals.

Once one learns to differentiate between hearing and listening this particular fear of not being loud enough will disappear. For while force and pressure diminish the sound volume of any violin (especially a really fine one) the search for overtones in the pitch will ensure a rich carrying quality.

Finally, the use of the inner ear will not only provide the music with colour and imagination, but it will help the player to stop thinking and worrying about himself, and after a while the question of 'Am I loud enough' has no chance even to arise.

2. The fear of not being fast enough

CAUSES
1. Rigidity throughout the whole body.
2. Lack of co-ordination between left hand and right hand.
3. Vertical finger pressure on the fingerboard and on the bow.
4. Enlarged, aggressive movements in the bowing arm and in the left hand action.

1. The release of physical blockages.
2. The application of a central point of co-ordination through the control of the left-hand action.
3. The awareness of the flow of time.
4. Economy of movements.

The fear of not being fast enough is especially pervasive in semi- or demi-semi-quaver passages, scales or arpeggios, runs and string crossings. Many players in their anxiety to overcome the feeling of rigidity (if not total paralysis) when confronted with a fast passage, tend to enlarge their strokes (often without being aware of it) or enlarge their left-finger action, and sometimes they do both. But as the quick, diffused movements between the bowing hand and the left-finger action only enhance their feeling of rigidity ("the two hands coming apart" to quote another violinist) they have no alternative but to take the bit between their teeth and run for it. And only those who have experienced riding on a runaway horse can fully appreciate the terrifying lack of control in a runaway passage.

This particular fear is especially strong in players who play from outside inward—i.e. whose bow motivation is in their fingers and wrist and whose left-hand technique consists of a vertical finger action. The antidotes to this—the inside-outward energy impulses, the elimination of the violin-hold, bow-hold as such, the 'giving' hand position, the lateral finger action, the co-ordinated bowing arm —have all been discussed in the section of this book dealing with the physical aspect of stage fright.

What we want to achieve now, through the application of the suggestions and exercises laid down in those chapters, is a central point of control, which has the power to create a total state of co-ordination. The first and foremost prerequisite of fast playing is co-ordination with a central point of direction which has the power to synchronize not only the physical actions, but also the workings of the mind.

This central point of direction which has the power to create total co-ordination of mind and body, lies in the naming of the notes. The importance of the naming of the notes has been touched upon already (see the exercises for the rhythmic pulse p. 19, the exercises for ear training on p. 73 and all the exercises in *The Twelve Lesson Course*), but its power of synchronizing mind and body has not yet been explained. But before going any further it is important to understand that our whole existence in our everyday life from babyhood onwards is based on constant identification of objects.

When a child learns that the word table means a particular object, a whole lot of information such as its shape, size and function are included in that one word. It is the same with names. We might know fifty people called Johnny, but any given Johnny we happen to think of will contain all the necessary information relating to him—the general shape of his figure, his voice, his personality. It is impossible for us to think of his hair, his voice or the colour of his eyes alone. It is his name that contains and centralizes all the physical and mental characteristics that we associate with him. Even when, for example, we see a pair of beautiful eyes belonging to some unknown person on the street or in a shop, we still identify the eyes by referring them to a 'woman', 'man', 'child', etc.

So is it with music. Here the accumulated information relating to each note is aural, visual and tactile. But here too, as in everyday activities, it is the name of the note which will synchronize all this information.

If our rhythmic impulse is unhampered (see p. 19), if our pitch is sensitive (p. 73) and our inner earimaginative (pp. 76-80) our tactile responses will be quite different when playing a 'C' in Beethoven from when playing a 'C' in, say, Shostakovitch. But all this will be realized without any conscious physical effort on our part if all the accumulated aural, visual and tactile information is centralized into the naming of the notes. In fact, one of the deepest causes of stage fright is just this, that one tries to achieve the desired musical effects through conscious physical efforts. And as so many players know, the more one tries, the less it works.

"Too often the physical pattern is the following: written notes, sounding the notes on an instrument, auditive perception and possible correction" says Kodaly. "On the other hand, the right course is the reverse; written notes, imagined sounds, implementation. In such a process there is hardly anything to be corrected. Beware of the actual concept of the notes becoming connected with an instrument or its handling. The aural image must live free and independent of any material association. This can be

82

achieved by reading the music through sol-fa . . . we breed agile fingers, but in most cases the spirit plods on leaden limbs to pursue the flying fingers, although in actuality the spirit must go first."*

In my experience using the letter names for the notes gives just as good results as using sol-fa (see p. 75). At first one ought to identify every sharp and flat, i.e. by saying F♯, B♭ etc., but later on one can abbreviate to just 'F' or 'B' or whatever the case may be, the mind having first firmly grasped the key.

EXERCISES (1)

It is interesting to note that many players who have not been trained from the beginning to identify the notes find it very difficult to say the names of the notes and seem extremely reluctant to acquire the habit. This is especially true when the concept of notes has been connected in the player's mind only with a finger action on the fingerboard with hardly any (or no) sensory, aural and imaginative perceptions. They may even find notation aloud difficult and when they are asked to do it, they remind one of a child not yet used to reading words.

For such players it is advisable to read music aloud every day as a matter of course, but only for a few minutes at a time, with two or three minutes' increase after every second or third day. This practise should be just plain reading without rhythm, singing or musical imagination. *This is merely for the eyes to get consciously used to notation information.*

> We find that the reading of a musical sequence away from the piano is far more effective than actually trying it with our hands on the keyboard. †

1. Follow the reading exercises by *singing* the same notes (within your octave range) with their names still without the rhythmic pulse or musical imagination. *This is for the ears to get consciously used to notation information.* Then add the rhythmic pulse by clapping and singing the same notations as before. And now

*Helga Szabo on *The Kodaly Concept of Music Education*, Boosey and Hawkes, London, 1969.
†*New Pathways To Piano Technique*, by Luigi Bonpensiere, The Philosophical Library, New York, 1953.

go over the same notes but add the appropriate finger action (still without the violin) to your reading and singing with the rhythmic pulse. But the finger action should be conceived only as a reaction, a mere follow through of the visual and aural concepts of the notes.

This exercise of singing with the rhythmic pulse while only miming with the left-hand finger action is very important, because it will help the finger action to get used to the notation information through the lead of the aural and visual images. It will also help eliminate the hard tactile concept between the fingertip and fingerboard—the enemy of all co-ordination and one of the greatest obstacles to fast playing.

Then be sure to say the names of the notes aloud a fraction before playing them on the violin. *This is for the touch to get used to the notation information in its proper sequence.* This way the visual, aural, and sensory information becomes united into one response, the naming of the notes. Naturally when identification becomes a habit, one does not need to say the names of the notes aloud. They will be embedded in the mind. And as the mind works faster than lightning, identification will be made at an incredible speed which eventually becomes the same natural process as the identification of people and objects around us (with all the subsidiary information relating to them).

So the sequence of co-ordination is: 1. identification (the naming of the notes containing aural, visual and sensory information); 2. Response of the left-finger action to the identification; 3. Responses in the right arm movements to the lead of the left hand (for this it is imperative that there are no blockages in the bow-hold, and elbow joint and that the whole bowing arm is based on motion and balance), without any conscious effort on the part of the player.

Scales, arpeggios, Sevcik Op. 1 No. 2 (position work) and Op. 8 (shifts) are especially useful exercises for saying the names of the notes aloud. But it cannot be emphasized enough that the naming of the notes is not an empty drill, and that it can fulfil its function as the central point of co-ordination only if the visual, aural, sensory, and tactile information is well established. Because if the identification of notes contains all this information (eventually on a subconscious level) the mind is so occupied transmitting these messages to the left hand, and the left hand is so busy receiving them (triggering off the right arm movements as well) that the player has no time left to think of himself. And with the elimination of the self "the physiological intelligence", to quote Huxley again, "is almost incapable of making a mistake".*

The other major point which has great curative value in eliminating the fear of not being fast enough is a concept of the flow of time. Time as we understand it has no beginning and no end. The adjectives 'fluid', 'mobile', and 'momentary' apply to the flow of time as they applied to the nature of sound (see p. 40). And in order to get rid of the fear of not being fast enough, it is essential that the central point of direction co-ordinating mind and body (the naming of the notes) becomes fused with the concept of the flow of time as well.

Imagine the flow of time as a strip of floor continuously on the move (as they have for luggage at airports) and then imagine stepping on and off it in rapid succession. If our footwork is hard and forceful, there is a terrible jar throughout the body each time we step on and off this strip—if we can maintain an upright position at all. Now, if you could endow the fingerboard in your mind with the same mobility as the continuously flowing strip, you'd realize that there is the same kind of physical jar throughout the body when the fingers hit the string. And then you would also realize that it is this continuous jolt to the flow of time that makes fast playing a seemingly impossible task. But, (to go back to the idea of the travellator, as this strip is called) if our footwork is light and follows the flow of the movement (as a result of total co-ordination throughout the whole body) there is a wonderful feeling of ease with a sense of being carried along. Then compare this gliding movement on the travellator to the sliding action of the fingers on the fingerboard (see p. 44).

This image has helped a lot of people to understand better that fast playing does not depend on hard working, aggressive finger action, but that speed comes as a natural process only if the flow of time is not continuously disturbed by the jolting blockages of a vertical finger action on the fingerboard.

Another major requisite of total co-ordination in fast playing is economy of movement. As was said before, the fear of not being

*Foreword to Bonpensiere, *op. cit.*

85

fast enough is especially rampant during semi- or demi-semi-quaver passages. This is due to the fact that many violinists tend to play these passages in the upper half of the bow with rapid opening and shutting of the elbow-joint. As this rapid elbow movement requires an extra grip of the bow, it often creates fatigue (if not pain) in the forearm and in the muscle between the thumb and the index finger, which, needless to say, is a great hindrance to music-making in general and to fast playing in particular.

So it is important to understand that if we wish to ride with the flow of time, economy of movement is absolutely essential. And in order to achieve this, the most natural place for the semi- and demi-semi-quaver passage is in the middle (by balance) of the bow where the elbow does not need to open and shut (see *A New Approach to Violin Playing*, pp. 48-53).

EXERCISES (2)

1. For best results, it is advisable to go over again the exercises for the quaver strokes in the lower half of the bow (see pp. 33-34) first of all without the bow. Then for the semi-quaver strokes, reduce the sideways swing of the upper arm (from the shoulder socket) to a microscopical self-propelled motion, "as if to nudge your neighbour" to quote another player.

2. Do this rápid sideways swing from the shoulder socket in groups of four as if playing on the violin but still without the bow. Say 'ta-ta-ta-tum' in a loud voice and allow the swing of the arm to respond to the direction of the vocal 'ta-ta-ta-tum'. At first it is advisable to stop for quite a long time between the groups. One is then able to anticipate the feeling of the sideways swing from the shoulder socket before each group. Then gradually reduce the time of stopping, until the groups are completely linked together. But even then, for real speed, it is most important to feel, think and pulse in groups of four. Make sure of the weightless, wing-like sensation in the arm (see pp. 30, 33), and that the sideways swing from the shoulder socket is a totally self-propelled, pendulum-like motion. The weightless, wing-like sensation in the arm is especially important in fast playing because a downward pressure with the bow on the string creates the same disturbance (both in

86

the flow of time and in the flow of sound) as does the vertical finger action on the fingerboard.

I have found that for many players this is much easier to achieve if the self-propelled motion is not connected in their minds with the bow-strokes at all. This again is most obvious in group work or at a master class, because while it is quite evident to those who watch whether the movements of the player are self-propelled or artificial, it is much more difficult for the player himself to differentiate. For, as was said before, in many cases the very thought of having to handle the bow is enough to create a certain amount of anxiety.

This is why it is so important to establish this movement in groups of four (to begin with) without the bow. Only when this is achieved, try the same movements on the open strings with the bow in hand. Make sure you maintain the weightless, wing-like arm position which is only possible if there is no bow-hold as such (see pp. 30, 33).

In extremely rapid groupings, the sideways swing from the shoulder socket is reduced to such an extent that it may become totally invisible and the only thing one can see is a movement in the fingers. However, as long as the feeling of a sideways swing in the shoulder socket is maintained, the movements in the fingers will only be a follow-through of this feeling. The problem of rigidity arises only when the finger movements on the stick become the actual activators of this stroke.

The sideways twist of the left fingers at string crossing is another impediment to the economy of movement in fast playing. And the same is true of the stretching, rigid fourth-finger action (see pp. 48-50). To attain economy of movement, especially at string crossings, it helps to imagine that the four strings are really only one broad string, so that there are no spaces between them and the fingers need not cross from one string to another. Imagine that the action always remains the same, from a back to forward slide; from the direction of the scroll towards the bridge (see p. 44), and you will find that the fingers will always go to the right string without the need of any twist at all. Also, as the motivation of the finger action is in the base joints (see *A New Approach to Violin Playing*, pp. 29, 30), the best way to gain speed is to reduce

87

the movements of the base joints to the bare minimum.
Mazas No. 5 or No. 6, Fiorillo, No. 11 or No. 12, or Kreutzer
No. 2 are good examples for practising fast passages.

(a) Sing the first two bars of any of the above exercises giving the
notes their names in groups of four (within the range of your
voice and with the help of the piano, or with the help of
plucking it on the violin).

(b) Put your left hand in front of you with the palm facing downward, as if playing the piano. Make certain that your wrist is
flexible and that the fingers are light and are gently curved in
every joint. Then say the names of the notes in groups of four
as fast as you can. You need not sing them this time. For
example the Kreutzer No. 2 would go like this

Make sure that each time you say the names of the notes in
these groups, the appropriate base joint moves with each
note within the group as if playing the notes on an imaginary
piano—with the thumb playing the open string. Make certain
that the wrist remains feather-light and that there is no feeling
in the fingers at all—that the motivation is from the base
joints.

3. Continue with this exercise line by line. Sing each group first and
then connect the saying of the notes with the movements in the
base joints so they become one and the same action.

4. Try the same exercise on the violin. Make sure that the bow is
placed on the string on its middle (by balance) and that it is resting on the string. Wait as long as you like between the groups.
But make certain that you say the names of the notes aloud with
the left-hand base joints reacting with the appropriate movements
in the 'giving' hand position. This way there should be no fingerboard idea in your mind and no pressing sensation in the fingertips.
Make sure that the sideways swing in the right shoulder socket
is only a reflex action to the rapid, cat's-paw-like movement of
the left base joints.

5. The next step is to say the names of a group of notes before you actually play them, but with such authority that the playing itself becomes a mere reflex action. It is best to practise this on scales in groups in legato bowing.

Let us take a three octave scale in G major with the notes grouped in triplets, each group to be slurred on the same bow. Get into playing position with the bow resting on the string. Say in rapid succession g a b and then let the playing respond with the same rapid 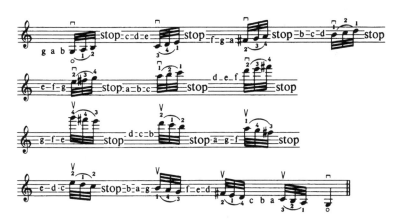 with the utmost economy of movement, so the left fingers hardly move and the length of the bow is minimal. Stop. Make sure you leave the bow on the string so it can continue with the same down slur stroke. Then say c d e and play ♪♪ continuing the down stroke. Stop. Say f g a (as an abbreviation for F♯) play it, ♪♪ etc., until you reach the top octave 'G'. Then continue with the exercise, coming down the scale with an up-stroke.

An accent at the beginning of each group means that there is too much finger pressure on the bow, and that the motivation of the stroke is not far enough removed from the arm.

89

6. Practise the arpeggios, dominant and diminished sevenths, the broken thirds and the chromatic scales in the same way.

It has been proved over and over again that once the player learns to centralize himself through this simple action of saying the names of the notes aloud in rapid successive groups, and learns to react to it with the same rapid (but with utmost economy of movement) left hand action (to which the right arm responds with equal rapidity in its economy of movement) the fear of not being fast enough soon disappears. In fact 'fast playing' as such will cease to exist. Instead, there will be a wonderful feeling of riding on the flow of time and being carried on by the speed of the music.

3. The fear of memory lapse

CAUSES
1. Rigidity throughout the body.
2. Reliance on mechanical, repetitive memorization.
3. Lack of co-ordination between the left-hand action and the bowing arm.
4. Anxiety caused by technical passages.
5. Anxiety caused by the inflated 'self'.

CURES
1. The release from physical blockages.
2. The division of each piece into sections.
3. The identification of the notes within each section through singing, and miming with the rhythmic pulse before playing it on the violin.
4. The alive *lead* of the left-hand control with the bowing arm responding.
5. The elimination of the 'self' through a systematic training of the mind.

The fear of memory lapse is the sum total of both the physical and mental anxieties. It is interesting to note that these breakdowns almost always occur when there is a special technical difficulty—a fast passage full of string crossings, an arpeggio run full of shifts, or a change in the rhythmic pattern, to mention only a few. And the worst part is that these breakdowns tend to occur only when playing in public. They hardly ever occur when playing at home.

The reason for this is that many players memorize only through their fingertips; one cannot deny that this finger-tip knowledge does work up to a point. That is—it works while playing at home. But the moment the player is exposed to any stresses and strains, i.e. an examination, audition or public performance, the fingertips do not have the necessary physiological authority to carry him through. Even if they had the authority, the negative thought process familiar to most of us when playing for other people would be enough to stop them from functioning properly. "Am I in tune"?, "am I loud enough?", "am I fast enough?", not to mention "am I good enough?", are sufficient barriers to break down the workings of any memory just when one needs it most. And trying to prevent these or similar thoughts by saying "I must not think of myself" will be, as we know only too well, totally useless. In fact, a negative thought process (because of the destructive elements it contains) is among the most deep-rooted anxieties.

I myself have never met a human being who is not endowed with a fair share of self-doubt, even in the best of circumstances. Which of us is certain of himself? Or who would not like to create a good impression, even at a bus stop? As it happens, most people look on these feelings of inferiority as a mere lack of confidence and are able to overcome them quite successfully. But when it becomes inflated, when this self-doubt becomes more than a normal part of one's make-up, then it is time to do something about it. As far as violinists are concerned, this inflated self-doubt has a way of attacking even the best players at the most unexpected moments on the concert stage. And the more sensitive the player is, the more he is exposed to it. And almost inevitably the first thing that suffers is his memory.

It would make an interesting book if one could collate the thoughts of people during a performance. As far as I can make out, anything goes from: "I don't sound good tonight", "will I make that high 'A' on the 'E' string", and "why does that woman wear that silly hat" to "I wish I were dead".

In order to prevent such thoughts, it is essential to establish a focal point of direction which has the power to centralize the mind into a systematic and constructive thought process. Obviously the more the player is exposed to physical tensions, the more difficult it is to centralize the mind. Therefore, here too (as it was with all other aspects of stage fright) the physical side of violin playing must first be put in order. It is most important that total motion and balance throughout the whole body, together with the inside-outward rhythmic impulses, should be well established before even attempting to play from memory. Then comes the training of the mind, which includes ear training (for the hearing of the pitch see pp. 73-74), and the training of the inner ear, the anticipatory listening to the quality, the musical imagination (see pp. 76-80), and the ultimate achievement of constant identification (see pp. 81-85—on the naming of the notes).

Now just as the physical side of playing should always be directed from inside outward (in order to avoid technical breakdowns) it is of paramount importance that memorization is conceived in the mind before it is transmitted through the fingers (see the reference to Kodaly, p. 82).

'Playing by heart' is an expression one would do well to adopt. Kreisler provides the epitome of this concept of the mind receiving and the fingers only transmitting. The anecdotes about his mental capacity are legendary. The following one was told by Michael Raucheisen, one of his pianists.

> When we arrived in Tokio we found the Japanese attached special impor-
> tance to sonatas. During the eight performances at the Imperial Theatre
> of Tokio, Kreisler was expected to perform virtually the entire existing
> sonata literature. I still remember as though it has taken place today,
> how Kreisler had an inquiry addressed to all musical Europeans there,
> as to whether, perchance, they had any sonatas for violin and piano in
> their libraries, so that we might fill all eight evenings with them. Kreisler
> had, of course, not prepared for such an unusual situation. Imagine,
> eight different programmes! And yet, one—I repeat—one rehearsal
> sufficed and Kreisler played the sonatas which he had not had on his
> repertoire for many years, by heart without a single flaw of memory,
> before this select international public.

I never have any trouble memorizing, (to quote Kreisler himself), "I know the music so well that I do not even keep the violin part. In fact I do not possess any. I study the part from the orchestral or piano score, I get it into my head with its accompaniment. It is all mental."*

Of course everybody's capacity to memorize is different, though according to some medical circles our mind is retentive by nature. That is, everything we hear, see or experience is carefully stored away in our minds for keeps, ready to use if we only knew how to release it. One of the most interesting examples of this theory is the story of the little servant girl in Germany, who had concussion and was in a coma for a considerable time. When she came to, she had no idea who she was, where she was or where she came from. All she could remember was the first few sentences of Homer's *Iliad* which she kept on repeating in perfect classical Greek, though she herself was completely illiterate. So, naturally, there was a considerable stir in the medical world when they found out that she had been employed by a professor of Greek whom, apparently, she had overheard teaching while she was cleaning.

But be that as it may, whether the player is quick or slow to memorize does not really matter, so long as the ever-looming threat of memory lapses on the stage can be cured. The release from physical tensions with systematic training of the mind seemed to be of great help to all players alike.

EXERCISES

I am sure that the following suggestions will seem obvious to many experienced violinists, but I think they will be the first to agree that a book of this nature would not be complete without such exercises.
1. Sit down with the music to be memorized, but without the violin and bow. If the music is not familiar, or perhaps not known to you at all, conceive it first with the inner ear (see pp. 76-80). Make certain that you are aware of every single clue relating to the music that the composer indicates. Make the composer (if he is dead) into a living personality in your mind. Imagine you know him and that he is a friend of yours. How would he like you to

Fritz Kreisler, by Louis P. Lochner, Rockliff, London, 1951.

93

play his music? What does he want to say with it? What would he want it to sound like? Train yourself to hear the music as clearly as if it were actually being played. Always look at the score (not only your part). If the music is familiar you are half way to knowing it already.

2. Divide the piece into sections, either phrase by phrase or theme by theme. Mark the sections in the music with a pencil either as (a), (b), (c) or (1), (2), (3), etc.

3. Look at the fingering and see if you agree with what is printed in the music. Does it help the musical ideas? Or is it approached only technically? What a difference it can make to the meaning of a piece of music when a theme is played on one string all through or when a string crossing is just in such and such a place. What about the bowing? Do the indications help to underline the wishes of the composer? Are they done by him or by an editor? If they are done by an editor, who is he? What nationality? What period? Do you agree with him?

4. Sing the first section, if necessary with the help of a piano (giving the notes their names), within the range of your voice and with the rhythmic pulse. If there is no piano, help yourself by plucking the melody on the violin (not playing it yet). If the piece is full of double stops, find the leading voice within the double stops, and sing those.

5. Put the music on the stand and play the first section, but only with an imaginary violin and bow, while singing it, naming the notes with a very powerful rhythmic pulse all through the body. Make certain that you really feel there *is* a violin and a bow and that all your movements are as real and accurate as if you were really playing. It is interesting to see how many players are unable to move at all if there is no violin and bow in their hands. This kind of work is especially useful at Lecture Demonstrations or at Group Teaching, because it accentuates the physical blockages much more dramatically than any amount of talk could.

6. Turn away from the music and play the section, still without the violin and the bow, but still singing and saying the names of the notes with the fingers and bow responding. If your memory breaks down, turn to the exact spot in the music where the memory lapse occurred. Make a careful mental note of the reason

for the lapse. Is it a sequence? Is it repeated? How many times is it repeated? What happens at the last repeat which leads on to the continuation? Be very patient and go over the section each time there is a lapse, giving yourself more and more information, but still playing only on an imaginary violin and bow. If you have rests, sing the part of the accompaniment.

7. Play the section now with the violin and the bow looking at the music but make sure you say the names of the notes to yourself while playing it. If there is a difficult shift, double stop, string crossing, etc., take these out of context and, with the help of the appropriate suggestions and exercises relating to the problem either in this book or in *A New Approach to Violin Playing* and *The Twelve Lesson Course*, release the physical tensions. It is important to realize that one problematic interval can affect the whole line of music around it. So learn to be able to spot these problematic intervals instantly. It will save a lot of time and a lot of useless (often soul-destroying) repetitive practice.

8. Play the section again from the music, saying the names of the notes to yourself, but this time be prepared for the problematic spots well ahead of time to prevent all possible physical tensions.

9. Turn away from the music and play it from memory. But make sure you turn completely away. Many players are in the habit of glancing constantly at the music which means that they are relying on their eyes and not on their memory. And so it is inevitable for a sense of anxiety to set in when the music is not there any more to be glanced at. But as before, if there happens to be memory lapse, turn back to the music, find the exact spot and be aware of why it happened. Then try again.

10. Go through the piece, section by section, the same way. If you find memorizing like this difficult at first, don't do more than one section a day. Your mind may need some time to get used to these new demands. Don't ever force it, but go at it patiently and systematically. Start all over again each day as if you have never worked on the piece before. Add an extra section each day until you have gone through all the sections.

11. Mix up the sections. Make each section an independent unit in your mind as if it were quite separate from the other sections. You ought to be able to start at section seven or at section five

as easily as at section one. In fact, if there is only a little time available for practise, it is advisable to work only on one given section each day.

12. Learn to play the piece in backwards order section by section, i.e. Play section 'd' (if you have decided on this kind of indication instead of on numbers) then section 'c', section 'b', and finally section 'a'.

This backwards way of playing from memory is a most important point. It prevents fatigue setting in, which often happens towards the end of a piece if one is used to playing it always from the beginning. It provides the mind with an equally fresh attitude at the end of a performance as at the beginning.

The learning of a piece through this total co-ordination of mind and body not only helps the player to release the physical tensions when on the concert stage, but also enables him to give full vent to his musical imagination through an authoritative thought process. And the power of communication becomes a constant sense of enjoyment and development.

4. The power of words

When dealing for any length of time with the causes and cures of stage fright, it becomes increasingly evident that the mental attitudes are as important, if not more so, than the physical side of playing. Often, when a person seems quite unable to release his tensions even when the movements are correct, using a word which creates a feeling of harmony and peace in him affords immediate results. Now, obviously these reactions are highly individual and in most cases totally subconscious. A word which may make all the difference to one player may not have any meaning at all to another. But there are a handful of words which I have found create similar reactions in most players. These can be divided into two categories: words which arouse tension and anxiety and words which create ease and flexibility. Some of these words have already been mentioned in the previous chapters when dealing with the physical aspects of stage fright. However, as they play such an important role in the creation of anxieties or in a state of well-being, it is worth drawing a clear and concise division between them.

The words 'hold', 'grip', 'pull', 'push', 'hit', 'press', 'stretch', 'vibrato', 'jump', 'listen', 'concentrate', 'good', 'bad', 'loud', create a certain amount of tension in almost every player. The words 'hold' and 'grip' relate to the violin hold and bow grip or to 'holding on' to something, most often to a note, especially when it is a long note. The static images of these words cannot help but create a tendency for localized, segmented efforts, i.e. pressing with the chin into the chin rest (p. 20), or holding on to the bow with the fingers and stiffening the arm through a long stroke (see pp. 28, 30). The words 'push' and 'pull' create the image of finger motivation of the bow, which by its proximity to the string disturbs the sound and the flow of the rhythmic pulse (see p. 19). 'Stretch' refers to the left-hand finger action, mostly to the fourth finger, causing tensions in the hand, thumb and wrist (especially at string crossings) (pp. 48, 50). The words 'hit' and 'press' cause rigidity in both hands, while the word 'jump' refers to shifts and creates the image of an endless fingerboard with all the anxieties concerning intonation (see pp. 62-67).

However, it is the image of vibrato which seems to create the most unfortunate word association. To many players it represents an oscillating movement, a 'shake' on its own, quite separate from tone production and intonation. And in order to oscillate on the note, they press into the string with their finger even more than they would otherwise, often without being aware of it. The conflict between the rigid feeling this creates and the image of beauty the vibrato stands for, can be one of the major causes for stage fright. The same applies to the words 'good' and 'bad' which help to accentuate the existing self doubts. And of course the word 'loud' can arouse almost more than anything else a static physical response (see the chapter on the fear of not being loud enough). Other qualitative words such as 'listen' or 'concentrate' cause constant concern with the self and hinder the flow of subconscious transmission, the 'let it happen' artistic communication.

97

On the other hand 'rest', 'nestle', 'cradle', referring to the violin hold; 'soft', 'satin', and 'silk' when referring to its texture; 'swing', 'slide', 'fan', 'spread', 'cuddle', 'curl', relating to the left hand action; 'rest', 'open', 'close', 'fly', concerning the bowing arm, create in most players an instant response of release.

Words like 'move', 'flow', 'give', 'love', 'release', 'pulse', 'through', 'unite' tend to be of great curative value for stage fright when applied at the right moment, because they are associated with harmonious activities. For that matter (perhaps unbeknown to the player), the different associations of the words 'power' on one hand and 'force' on the other, can be the making or breaking of stage fright during a performance. The word 'force' is often connected with violence in one's mind and if not with violence, with intense effort. So the mental process of 'I must force myself to play well' will only result in setting up additional stresses and strains with subsequent static reactions. The word 'power', on the other hand, tends to be associated with an authority greater than oneself, with an endless supply of energy and movement. So the usage of words which create release plays an important part in the elimination of stage fright.

5. *The power of imagination*

It is the same with the imagination. The images applied to help to release tension and anxiety also rely on the connotation of words, i.e. 'total motion and balance', 'playing through the instrument', 'the giving left-hand position', 'the inside-outward rhythmic impulse', all indicate a continuous transmission which, after all, is the major goal of every musician.

In fact, the power of imagination turns out to be one of the greatest, if not the greatest, asset in the elimination of stage fright. As was said before, sometimes when the player understands quite well how he can attain physical release, it does not necessarily mean that he can actually achieve it, if his inner hold-up (or self-doubt) is too strong. However, it has been proved over and over again that if the player learns to activate his imagination with positive ideas, his self-doubt tends to disappear and then he obtains the desired physical release as well. For best results, it helps if the images are as vivid as possible. For example, for many players the weightless, wing-like sensation in the arm concerned with the violin hold (see p. 22) becomes much more real when I emphasize the lightness by blowing against the inside of my own upper arm (in the violin bow-hold position) which instantly responds with a sideways swing. Almost invariably the player's arm (which may have been as rigid as a board before) will respond in the same way when it is blown against.

Also, the idea of the violin being alive tends to become much easier to accept when it is emphasized that its parts are named after the human body, i.e. the back, belly, ribs and the neck. It is also a great help when the player learns to identify the neck of the violin with his own neck and imagines how it would feel if somebody pressed a thumb against his vocal cords and said 'sing'. From that it is only a step to imagining that a rough, harsh sound means that the violin is actually in pain.

For some people it helps to imagine that instead of the neck of the violin, a sponge is placed in their 'giving' hand position. Then as their fingers (and thumb) curl around the imaginary sponge, they imagine water dripping through between the roots of their fingers. When they apply the same sensation with the neck of the violin in their hands, they feel that sound is oozing through between the root of their fingers. For other people it helps if they can imagine that the neck of the violin is a delicate bird which they manipulate to sing.

Another way to emphasize the idea that the player and his instrument are only the means of transmitting music is to associate the left arm with an empty river bed into which flows a multi-coloured substance—the sound—from the source which is the body. This is driven by the rhythmic pulse until in the end it spurts through the roots of the fingers. But the most helpful idea has proved to be to compare the rhythmic pulse with the waves in the sea, except that in music these imaginary waves generate in the body and surge through the left shoulder socket, arm, hand, and fingers, sweeping away all blockages, while the right arm responds to this powerful ride of the rhythmic pulse.

It has been pointed out over and over again that it is always the left arm, hand and fingers with which these imaginary exercises are concerned.

The imaginative exercises relating to the bow are always secondary and are concerned with reflex actions responding to the lead of the left hand. But this is impossible to achieve while there is even the slightest tension in the bow hold. As the bow-grip is the cause of one of the most prevalent anxieties in violin playing and is one of the major causes for stage fright (see the chapter on the fear of the trembling bowing arm, p. 28) it is important to pay special attention to the release of this grip. However, here too, when the mental anxiety is so strong that all physical attempts at release fail, the use of the imagination often comes to the rescue. For example, many players were helped in releasing their bow-hold by the image of 'layers' of rest—their feet resting on the floor (and at the same time supported by it), their violin resting on the collar-bone, the bow resting on the string (supported by it underneath), and their hand resting on the bow. Then this image of 'layers' of rest is combined with a buoyant, spongy sensation throughout the body with the sound flowing through the layers; like cream oozing out from between layers of cake placed on top of each other.

As this anxiety over the bow-hold often originates in childhood, it is interesting to see how this image can revert to the past and what comfort the association of sound with oozing cream affords even to those adults who are well advanced in years!*

The compound, the sum-total, of all these ideas is of course the transmission of music. The aim of all the physical and mental exercises in this book is for the player to become so saturated with sound and movement that he is virtually compelled to transmit them to other people. When a musician begins to feel that the whole of his being consists of music and is filled with music, the nightmare of stage fright is much less likely to trouble him again. And under such

*See *Education and the Imagination* by Ruth Mock, Chatto & Windus, London, 1970.

conditions the playing for people cannot help but become a natural and pleasureable occupation.

One of the best stories relating to spontaneous music-making is about Sir Thomas Beecham. He, like Kreisler, believed that the mechanical side of music-making did more harm than good and as a result often gave performances without any previous rehearsals. And when on such an occasion one of the wind players (who had a big solo part) complained that he did not know the music he was going to perform that evening, again without any rehearsal, Sir Thomas exclaimed "Is that so?" and then, brightening considerably, added with enthusiasm, "My dear fellow, you'll love it."

V

The Social Aspects of Stage Fright

1. The fear of not being good enough

1. *The fear of not being good enough*

CAUSES
1. The competitive attitude in our social system.
2. The 'strive to succeed' attitude in a competitive world.
3. The evaluation of one's personal worth according to the degree of success accorded by society.

CURES
1. To look on violin playing as a form of creative art instead of as a technical accomplishment.
2. To exchange the concept of 'good' and 'bad' in violin playing for a standard of physical comfort and also to assess the degree of one's success by the ability to transmit the music to the listener.
3. To eliminate the existing teacher-pupil relationship and replace it with a 'give' and 'receive' musical communication.

After the physical and mental aspects of the causes of stage fright, one basic cause still remains: the all-pervading competitive attitudes in our social system.

> Competitiveness is one of the predominant factors in social relationships. It pervades the relationships between men and women, between women and women . . . and perhaps most important of all, it pervades the family situation, so that as a rule the child is inoculated with this germ from the very beginning.*

I wonder if there is a child in the world who would not like to give pleasure to both his parents and his teacher if he only knew how. Parental approval gives him a sense of security and belonging. It is nice to be praised in a world which seems so full of complexities. Most parents consider their children as a reflection of themselves and cannot help showing their pride and pleasure when the child does something well. Even the most progressive parent who believes in total freedom of development, cannot help exuding a sense of pride in the achievement of his child. This sense of pride does not even have to be expressed in so many words for the child to be aware of it and to respond accordingly.

The Neurotic Personality of Our Time, by Karen Horney, W. W. Norton & Co. Inc., New York, 1937.

The trouble is that just as the parents cannot resist showing pride in their children's achievements, equally they cannot help projecting considerable anxiety for the child to do well, in fact to do just a little better than his contemporaries. Therefore, the child soon becomes aware that just trying to please is not quite enough. In order to get real approval from his parents and his teacher, he has to try to outshine his friends. So, from the very beginning, love and security in the child's mind is linked with rivalry and competitions.

> With the development of understanding of the meaning of competition and of awareness of one's own status as compared with others, there frequently come fears of loss of prestige, ridicule and failure.*

The problems begin when the child cannot fulfil these expectations. Then he is capable of doing almost anything just to get attention.

Goodness knows there is plenty of competition in the life of every ordinary child especially, for example, with the birth of a younger brother or sister, and most parents are familiar with the problems the new arrival creates in the first-born. However, most educated parents today are aware of this problem and they are able to lessen, and often completely to avoid its effects. Unfortunately, child psychology is hardly ever applied to the young violinist, and in the case of these young students, regardless of whether they are three, five, seven years old or what have you, the degree of their personal standing still depends on the degree of their achievement, or for that matter, the lack of it.

As if it were not enough to be gripped by fears that he may drop the violin and bow, that his fingers are too stiff to find the notes, that the violin may make an awful sound, that, in fact, the whole procedure won't add up to anything but acute discomfort, the child is already desperately struggling with competitive challenges.

Of course, he would like to play easily and well, if he only knew how. But unless he is among the rare naturals, he does not know how. The eternal 'good' and 'bad' which surround his everyday life as it is, loom up even larger when playing the violin.

"Don't you hear how well Johnny plays? Why don't you try to play as well as he does?"

Child Psychology, by A. T. Jersild, Prentice Hall Inc., New York, 1940.

"The reason Rosemary plays so well is that *she* practises every day, not like you."

Once I even heard a mother yell at her son, "Concentrate, Peter, concentrate!" Peter was aged three.

I have also noticed over and over again (of course there is always the exception) that a specially gifted child is much freer and responds much better if his mother is not present at the violin lessons. The mother can sit quite quietly in one corner, and even pretend to read, but without her even knowing it she almost always exudes anxiety for him to do well, especially when the child is working for an examination or a performance. On these occasions, in order to prove his worth, he is expected to play a great deal better than the other children or at least a little better. Without the parent being fully conscious of it, the degree of praise the child receives at home often goes hand in hand with the degree of his success in front of an audience, or in the marks the examiner allots him.

What is more, the problem of competitive success among violinists does not stop in childhood. If anything, it increases all through life until, especially if he is a performer, it becomes the symbol of his existence. Because of the nature of his career, the chances are that his success or failure compared with other players becomes the dominant criterion of his self-evaluation. It is not really surprising that under these conditions his worth as a personality is gauged by the degree of his achievement.

Anxiety has its counterpart in a sense of reflected glory. This is felt not only by parents. Many teachers seem even guiltier of projecting their personal anxiety on to their pupils, and guiltier still of basking in their pupils' successes. Hence the rivalry of the different violin schools and violin teachers. The hurt and fury caused when a pupil, especially a promising one, decides to leave and go to another teacher is too well known to be pointed out. It is enough to say that I have known cases of the teacher becoming ill when a pupil left him in order to study with someone else. According to an article about an international competition, a teacher actually shot himself when his pupil failed to win first prize.*

*'The Night the Violinist Lost his Way in a Bach Fugue', by Ian Cotton, *Sunday Times Magazine*, Oct. 1971.

Competitions of this sort of course epitomize all the horrors of stage fright, for the whole future of a young player may depend on such an occasion. It may make or break his career. If he is among the winners, his name becomes internationally known overnight and his career as a soloist is assured—alas, in many cases, only for a while. Even if he wins, the obsessive fear and anxiety experienced on such an occasion and the training that lead up to it, can damage him for life.

"It was fascinating to watch, after those eighteen years she described of agonizing study and emotional trauma", continues the article mentioned, depicting the winner, "this mass adulation pouring the life blood into the bruised and battered psyche of the soloist."

The tragedy is that in more cases than not the psyche has become too bruised and battered for it to withstand the rigours of a soloist's life. The article goes on to say: "For many performers the actual process of rendition is excruciating . . . the South African contestant has a face which seems to have been permanently twisted by experience . . ." "When I get on the platform," to quote some of the players themselves, "I get so nervous I feel physically sick. My knees are shaking and I can't trust my bow-arm." . . . "Thinking about everything . . . everything except being there and playing that music . . . anything so I can forget the jury taking notes every time I'm a semitone out of tune". But even if the psyche survives these conditions, the severity of such a training cannot help affecting, if not completely eliminating, the artistic creativity (the divine spark) the player may have had. And so even if he becomes a successful violinist it is unlikely that he can ever find fulfilment in becoming a creative artist. And the fear of not being good enough will tend to stay with him for the rest of his life.

The criterion of success goes hand in hand with the necessity of competitive attitudes in our society. "Strive to succeed" is not an unusual motto to see displayed in schools where the children are hardly out of kindergarten. 'To become successful' is an accepted goal and 'to be successful' is an accepted achievement in our social structure. But what many people are not aware of is that the word success is almost always connected with material achievement. While it is perfectly all right to say 'he is a successful business man', one would hardly refer to a person as a 'successful lover'.

Equally, while it is perfectly all right to speak of success in winning a match or getting a job, one would not put the writing of a poem or the painting of a picture in the same category. When one refers to an artist as a successful writer or painter, it merely implies a concept of his financial status, for the intrinsic value of creativity cannot be measured in terms of success. But unfortunately, because of the yearly examinations, auditions and competitions to which a violinist is constantly exposed, the criterion of success does not only become part of his life along with the businessmen and sportsmen, but often becomes the only goal he knows. And even then there is the realization that striving for success forms only part of his task, the other part is to learn how to keep it once it is achieved. For under these terms even when he manages to get to the top, he soon finds out that there is a constant threat to his stature from other players. It is the timeless story of Ibsen's Master Builder over and over again. No wonder that under these social conditions the fear of not being good enough, one of the basic causes for stage fright, is an ever-present problem.

The anxiety in striving for success tends to be at its worst when playing at auditions. One has some sort of choice in entering a competition or giving a recital, but there is no choice whatsoever about having to play at an audition if one wants a job. Or for that matter a student, however promising he may be, cannot expect to be admitted to a traditional institution or to be taught by a well-known personality, without an audition. This has been true throughout the history of violin pedagogy. These auditions usually demand from the aspiring student at least one concerto, a movement of unaccompanied Bach, a virtuoso piece or two (such as Lalo or Sarasate), études and scales. And as a great musical institution or the name of a great teacher is essential to the furtherance of his career, the outcome of these auditions is one of the most important landmarks in his development. If he succeeds, the prestige he gains is almost negligible in comparison with the gain in self-confidence and self-respect. Equally, if his nerves let him down, the chances are that he will never quite recover from a sense of being a failure.

One of the best descriptions of such an audition was given by Ruth Ray (one of the star pupils of Leopold Auer) at my Summer School in Dorset. When I realized who she was I asked her to give a talk

108

to the young people present. Though hers was, of course, a story with a happy outcome, she gave a most vivid description of the hours and hours of soul-destroying practise, nerves and heartaches that had preceded such an audition. It was interesting to note that the terrors, thrills and all the rest of the emotional and competitive gamut that encompassed the life of a prodigy in those days did not seem all that different from the conditions prevailing at present, despite all our knowledge about psychology.

In *The Violin and I* my own experiences as a child prodigy are also described—and one does not have to look far to find many other examples as well. But one does not even have to be a child prodigy to be exposed to these stresses and strains in the name of music-making. Even an ordinary little Johnny, who just loves playing his violin and does not particularly wish to shine, finds himself being put through the grades before he knows what has happened to him. Examinations are for his own good he is told—until he is convinced that they provide him with a goal, a reason for practising.

Obviously great teachers like Auer and Joachim and the great teachers of the present day exert an enormous influence over their pupils. The pity of it is that because of the audition system, a star teacher tends to accept only those students who are able to survive the strains of these auditions. The equally talented and often perhaps the even more creative and sensitive player, who cannot survive them, is apt to fall by the wayside. The competitive, 'strive to succeed' conditions allow only the fittest to survive. But the fittest for what? There is a story of Kreisler overhearing a small boy during a performance of Mischa Elman (who was noted for his sweet tone) whisper to his mother, "Mummy, I can play faster than him."

The fear of being exposed as not being good enough, or of perhaps not being able to sustain being good enough, has hampered the careers and sometimes ruined the lives of many fine violinists. For any existence which depends on competing with and being judged by one's fellow humans, cannot help but produce a morass of devastating self-doubt.

As one cannot change the social system, the question is how to deal with the problems created by it. As the saying goes, if you cannot beat them, join them. But with a difference. In other words, seeing that one cannot change the system of examinations, auditions and competitions, simply because there is no other workable system available, what one has to change is the attitude the system has created. There is no doubt that the problem of stage fright could be greatly reduced if, from the very beginning, violin playing were considered a form of creative art, rather than a technical accomplishment. How often does one come across a parent or a teacher who tells the child (and means it) how lovely the music is, how lovely the violin can sound, and what a giver of pleasure he is because he plays the violin?

As the idea of 'giving'—of transmitting something greater than oneself—is the essence of every artistic creativity, it is this idea that should be nurtured from the very beginning. If all the necessary examinations, auditions and competitions were channelized into a 'giving' process from the start, many of the physical and mental blockages which are such a problem at present would not exist.

It is a well known fact that before examinations even the best students are apt to be affected by nerves which affect their playing harmfully. The best example I know was a young boy aged eleven who, after a marvellous start on the violin, began to play out of tune and develop all sorts of physical blockages. For a while I could not fathom out what was wrong, because not only had he perfect pitch, but was one of the most agile children I have ever come across. Then it transpired that his housemaster, in return for allowing him to travel a hundred miles to London for his lesson every week, fully expected him not only to take the customary examinations in violin playing, but also to pass them with flying colours, (a) because he was my pupil, and (b) because it would glorify his particular house in school. And the examination, as it turned out, was imminent. I think that was the first time I realized how useless it would be to try to change the social system. It would have served no purpose to try to shield that child from the rigours of life, because sooner or later he would have had to be exposed to them. A protective, hot-house-like attitude did not seem the answer to the problem. So I explained that it was all very well for him to be nervous, but had he thought of the poor examiner? Of what a dreadful job it must be to listen to the same pieces over and over again, which are quaked through by nervous players day in and day out? "No," he said, rather startled, but obviously pleased at the notion of the dreaded examiner being in need of his compassion. By enlarging on this idea and by making it quite clear that I would not think him a better player even if he got distinction, and equally would not think him a worse player if he failed, as long as he tried to give as much pleasure to the examiner as he could, I managed to take away his fear of not being good enough. As a result the symptoms of anxiety, i.e. faulty intonation, stiff wrists, etc., disappeared and his playing, if anything, became better. And later when he showed me the examiner's comments which said among other things 'I enjoyed listening to you', I gave him a bag of sweets as a reward!

Needless to say the same training of behaviour is applied to adult players as well, regardless of whether they are amateurs or professionals. For it seems that childhood impressions of our competitive and success-chasing society are everlasting. It is interesting to note how even an amateur, often even the most sophisticated, intelligent and maybe eminent person, is apt to revert to childhood attitudes the moment his lesson begins. On the surface these players have nothing to be anxious about because their career and livelihood is well assured elsewhere, and they are supposed to play music only for pleasure. Yet, the moment their lessons begin, even if they happen to be close personal friends, sometimes maybe many years senior, they immediately look to you to scold or praise. They practically compel you to hold judgement on their ability in the role of a teacher. Just like many of the professional players, they are either so frightened of not doing well, or are trying so hard to do well, that they are quite unable to play as freely and with as much enjoyment as they would do at home.

I find that in order to eliminate the social causes for stage fright, it is necessary to try to eliminate the teacher-pupil relationship first. And as the teacher often stands for a parent figure as well (whom one tries to please in return for love) the attempt to eliminate this associative relationship often serves a double purpose.

There are three basic points which seem to help towards achieving this. One is to supplant the player's self-doubt and anxiety with such positive actions and thoughts that he has no time to think of himself. These points have been discussed at length with appropriate exercises in the two previous sections of this book, one dealing with the physical and the other with the mental aspects of stage fright. The second point is that instead of telling the player what to do or what not to do, i.e. 'flex your wrist', 'don't play so fast', I have learned to base the lessons on a mutual exchange of ideas. In other words, instead of giving an opinion in the capacity of a teacher, I try to make the player understand by making it as clear as I can why his wrist is stiff or his playing too fast. By discussion and demonstration it becomes evident that whatever the problem may be, it is not due to his personal short-comings but to a misconception of physical balances or mental attitudes, or perhaps both. What is more, he is asked to question every suggestion I may make, if he does not find the reasons for them clear enough. In fact, he is actually urged not to take anything at face value but to argue each point if he does not feel convinced.

This way the player learns to find out alone where and how he can help himself. And as he learns to help himself, the anxiety of having to test his ability in front of the teacher is eliminated (see *The Violin and I*). These discussions not only help to transform the teacher-pupil relationship into a working partnership, but they help to change all the anxieties connected with violin-playing into constructive activities.

Finally, I find that for the pupil to acquire these active thinking and playing habits, it is necessary to change the usual method of evaluation from being 'good' or 'bad' (which reflects on his own ability), to having a sense of well-being.

If the evaluation of his playing is based on whether he feels comfortable or not (which he knows can be controlled by physical balances and mental attitudes) the anxiety about his own image (of having to test his ability in front of the teacher) is slowly eradicated. For nothing can eliminate self-doubt quicker and better when playing the violin than a sense of physical well-being (see the chapter on the Hungarian gypsy violinist, p. 11).

Once this state of comfort (or at least the searching for it) is achieved, the next step is to try to transfer the teacher-pupil relationship (of judging and being judged) to one of an active artist-audience, a 'give' and 'receive' musical communication.

Of course this works both ways, because it is equally important that each time the teacher demonstrates something, it is he who 'gives' then and the pupil who 'receives'. It is very important that these demonstrations by the teacher do not stand for personal achievements either. The purpose of each demonstration is to show why a certain passage seems difficult and how it is possible to make it easy, and not how clever or superior the teacher may be.

As self-justification has no part in a 'give' and 'receive' musical relationship, the physical and mental attitudes acquired during the course of these lessons become the greatest factors in the elimination of stage fright. And by consciously establishing a natural outlet for musical communication as the one and only reason for violin playing, the development of most players becomes quite astounding.

The 'give' and 'receive' attitudes and sense of comfort as the basis of evaluation seem to work particularly well with children, especially when it is their turn to teach you. They learn to teach by touch.

"Your elbow is stiff."

"Now it is flexible."

"Now you clutch the violin."

"Now you don't."

"This is a nice sound."

"Why?"

"Because it has a ring."

"This is an ugly sound."

"Why?"

"Because it sounds hoarse"—"sandy" to use the expression of one child.

"When is the sound nice? When my elbow is stiff or when it is flexible?"

"Am I in tune? If not will you adjust my finger for me?"

"But I can't move your finger."

"Why?"

"It is too stiff."

"Why?"

"Because it is pressing into the string," etc., etc. So a lovely sound is associated with flexibility and comfort from the beginning. And the transference from 'this is good', 'this is bad', to 'this sounds nice', 'this does not sound nice', not only enhances the awareness of the pupil, but his musical development as well.

113

The vivid use of images, such as endowing the violin with life, and referring to the weightless arms which can float on air like the wings of a bird, the jolly major third, the sad minor third, the singing of notes with the clapping of the pulse, the connection between the names of the notes and a movement with the left fingers all help to ensure a creative attitude from the beginning. It takes away the burden of having to learn an instrument with the onus of having to do well. But the greatest help in connecting the imagination with that of the actual skill of playing is the miming of the movements without the violin and bow while singing the notes. This applies to the teacher as much as to the child.

"Can you hear the music through my movements?"

"No."

"Why?"

"Because you pulse three instead of two," or "Because you are not using the right fingers", etc.

I cannot emphasize enough how this kind of work helps to eliminate the competitive and 'strive to succeed' attitudes. In fact sometimes I actually tell a child who happens to be particularly highly strung that I don't mind how badly he plays as long as he tries to feel comfortable. And when he begins to do so and I begin to enjoy the music, even if the music happens to consist of open strings, there is a sweet for him at the end of the lesson. And eventually the feeling of comfort and his listener's enjoyment will stand for "playing well".

The changing of adults' attitudes is more difficult. This becomes especially evident during the Master Classes at my Summer School. My repeated requests of "please don't try to play well," meet with some astonishment at first as the victim (judging by his demeanour) stands up in front of everybody, ready to 'face the music', so to speak. I have never come across a violinist, however good he may be, who does not fear that his playing will fail him on such occasions.

Therefore, the whole Summer School is geared just to this. The elimination of stage fright underlies the whole programme of the School. All the work, from morning to night, is based on the principles of physical comfort and 'give' and 'receive' attitudes. The day is divided into two sessions. The morning classes deal with the physical aspects: the elimination of tensions and blockages by discussing, clarifying and demonstrating the causes and cures. It is always a great help when the standard of players is mixed, for there is great dramatic value for the advanced or professional player in seeing the release in a seemingly hopeless amateur—while for an amateur or for a beginner it is equally valuable to hear a startling improvement in an already fine violinist.

As these discussions and demonstrations are never aimed at an individual as such, but to the problems of all violinists and thus concerning everyone in the group, the competitive and 'strive to succeed' attitudes are replaced with a constructive and exhilarating atmosphere.

> The immediate results in their playing were so apparent that people stopped thinking about themselves and became interested in the nature of the problems instead.*

As the problems of one person apply to all the others (though maybe in different degrees) it becomes obvious that if that person can obtain release, so can they all. "The outside world stopped, and we became as intimate and involved with each other as if we were on a ship's voyage."†

In the afternoon there are the master classes. These serve to show that with the release of the physical tensions the musical imagination is released as well, and interpretation becomes a free-flowing creativity. It is at the master classes that the mental aspects of stage fright are not only unearthed and discussed but, by performing to the class, are integrated with the physical side of playing. However, one of the most important factors in the elimination of the personal challenges is the Festival. This Festival of Music is attached to the Summer School and provides public performances almost every evening in stately homes or in lovely old churches, or (for smaller invited audiences) in the school itself, where the less advanced players have a chance to perform as well. Based on the same principles as the morning and afternoon sessions (of the 'give' and 'receive' attitudes) these concerts help eliminate the gap between practising and performing. They become a sort of culmination of the day's work and provide the players with marvellous opportunities of

*The Violin and I.
†Ibid.

gaining practical experience in playing for an audience under these new conditions.

Another factor which seems to be of some importance is that the Festival is non-profit-making. All profits go to charity, which means that with the elimination of evaluations such as 'good' and 'bad', the financial side of having to succeed also becomes extinct. Instead, there is an over-all interest in raising as much money as possible for those who are less fortunate. This seems to give the players extra incentive to 'give' through the violin as well. As a result there is a wonderful aura of personal freedom in the air (the best of all possible cures for stage fright) with a natural bond of giving between artist and audience.

Also, there are constant examples of playing for the sheer pleasure of it by guest artists from all over the world.

> Purbeck folk were surprised at first to find celebrities like Sir Arthur Bliss or a conductor from the Metropolitan Opera House strolling down the village street. But they soon got used to the idea and to the musicians drifting into Kato Havas's place for rehearsals, in shorts and open necked shirts, straight from a swim or a ramble.*

Now it is obvious that this kind of arrangement is practicable only for short periods, in this case it lasts for one month every summer. But the combination of mental, physical and social releases which the player experiences during the course of his stay provide him with a working knowledge of the problems concerning stage fright. And needless to say this will be one of the most important aspects of his development. For only if one understands the causes can one apply the cures. And the physical and mental releases witnessed and experienced during class-work and during performances cannot help but make an impression on him to which he can refer back when necessary. Once a player learns to question why a shift or double stop passage does not work, and understands how it is possible to make it work, he will have much less time and energy to fear that he himself may not be good enough.

It is important to understand that stage fright does not leave one all at once. One cannot expect a life-long behaviour pattern to

*Eileen Elias, 'British Festivals', *Homes and Gardens*, Feb. 1971.

116

disappear overnight. In fact, as was said before, a certain amount of anxiety is a necessary part of our make-up (see p. 5). But if the player learns to release these anxieties into a free-flowing activity, it will enable him to give vent to his musical imagination much more when confronted with an audience than he would be able to do when playing at home. And this is what the training is all about—to turn stage fright into an advantage with the idea that 'giving', transmitting something greater than oneself, is the essence of all artistic creativity.

VI

Conclusion

1. The art of practising

2. Suggestions for: examinations
   auditions
   competitions
   performances

3. The salient points in practising

1. *The art of practising*

Few people realize that faulty practising is, more often than not, the deepest and greatest cause for stage fright. The trouble is that practising is seldom thought of in connection with music. Instead, it tends to be looked upon as repetitive muscular training for the strengthening of the fingers and the conditioning of the muscles. What is worse, many musicians cannot play at all (or think they cannot) unless they have practised for so many hours beforehand. And even if they have practised for months on end, five, six (or more) hours every day, and all day before the actual performance, they are still afraid that unless there is a chance to warm up their fingers all over again before going on the stage, they will not be able to play a note—which, alas, is not far from the mark. For usually the physical and psychological (not to mention the acoustical) conditions are so totally different between the hours spent in practising and the actual moment of performance, that these differences alone are enough to create stage fright and breakdowns. It is no wonder that the player tries to hang on to his instrument for safety.

"Probably the worst pressure on the competitors was the almost neurotic compulsion many of them felt to keep up a high daily average of practise," notes Mr. Cotton in his article in the *Sunday Times**, and goes on to describe how one of the competitors used to be roused from bed at five-thirty in the morning as a child so that she could put in her daily practise before school. And how another competitor, at one stage, was doing five or six hours a day on top of a full orchestra quota. At the competition itself according to the same article, "it was not unusual for the day to start at eight and finish at midnight or later and all the time between was spent (excepting meal breaks) in playing the violin."

The root of the problem is that if the physical actions concerning violin playing are artificially conditioned or (as in so many cases) forced, they do not afford any real assurance. Instead, the constant and recurring breakdowns at the same passages (in spite of the hours of practise) tend to envelop the player with a feeling of inadequacy.

*'The Night the Violininst Lost his Way in a Bach Fugue', by Ian Cotton, *Sunday Times Magazine*, Oct. 1971.

A MASTER CLASS AT THE SUMMER SCHOOL, DORSET

Photo by John Rutherford.

121

WITH SIR ARTHUR BLISS AFTER A FESTIVAL CONCERT, DORSET

Photo by John Rutherford.

122

IN THE RHONDDA VALLEY, WALES
Photo by K. D. Williams.

AT THE EASTMAN SCHOOL
OF MUSIC, NEW YORK
Photo by Louis Ouzer.

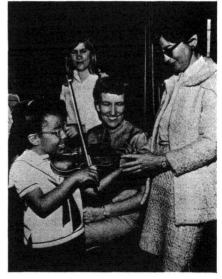

AT THE CHAPMAN SCHOOL OF
MUSIC, VIRGINIA
Photo by Harold Chapman.

AT FRESNO STATE COLLEGE,
CALIFORNIA
Photo by Mrs. Wilson Coker.

A COUNTRY HOUSE CONCERT AT THE PURBECK FESTIVAL
Photo by John Rutherford.

And to make things worse, once this feeling of insecurity is estab-lished the dependency on the hours of practice becomes even greater. The sense of guilt, when not fulfilling a pre-determined daily quota of practising is enough to send many a musician to the couch of the psycho-analyst. It is as if the mental suffering (so common among violinists) helped to expiate the guilt which arises from the feeling of inadequacy. "To rely on muscular habit, which so many do in technique, is indeed fatal" says Kreisler in his comments on prac-tising. "A little nervousness, a muscle bewildered and unable to direct itself, and where are you? For technique is truly a matter of the brain . . . how sad it is that in these days the emphasis is on how many hours one practises." Then he goes on to say how he met Kubelik one afternoon who had apparently been practising for twelve hours and his fingers were bleeding.

"When he played that night," observed Kreisler, "it was techni-cally a perfect performance, but yet it was a blank. I never practise before a concert. The reason is that practise benumbs the brain, renders the imagination less acute and deadens the sense of alertness that every artist must possess."*

This reliance on repetitive, muscular training can become such a burden that one tends to forget what a wonderful gift it is to be born a musician; that in fact the task lies not in the hours of practise but in learning how to appreciate this gift entrusted to us *which entails learning to love ourselves.* And how can one do this through finger exercises and through constant self-doubt? Especially when a certain amount of self-depreciation is actually encouraged because it is considered modesty; while the idea of loving oneself is often looked upon as being on the borderline of sin. But nowadays, more and more people (especially the young) realize that in loving oneself lies the secret in loving others.

In fact, when dealing with stage fright, the first thing one must set out to eliminate is the reason for self-depreciation and self-doubt. For how can a musician communicate the meaning of music (especi-ally when it comes to Mozart) unless he knows what love is all about? How can he 'give' unless he is free to love himself, his fellow beings and, most of all, his audience?

*Fritz Kreisler, by Louis P. Lochner, Rockliff, London, 1951.

125

In order to avoid all possible tendencies for mechanical practise, it is important to realize that the preparation of a sense of physical and mental well-being for the day's work is as necessary (if not more so) than the practising itself. This is especially true when the player is under strain because of a heavy schedule.

The best and most fruitful time for practising is first thing in the morning while the brain is still fresh. Even if it is no more than twenty minutes or half an hour. One hour is ideal, two hours are to be considered a luxury. And even when one is free to practise all day long, the time spent with the violin should not exceed four hours. But whatever time you have available, it is not the length of the practise that counts but its quality, most of all its 'first-thing-in-the-morning' regularity. This regularity is very important even if it has to be very early because of other commitments such as teaching, rehearsing, etc.

Of course the meaning 'early' is relative. It means something quite different to a person living in a city and to a farmer living in the country. A great deal also depends on what time one managed to get to bed the night before. But whatever 'early' may mean to someone who has difficulty in waking up (as so many people have), it is advisable to allow an extra half hour for the actual waking-up period. Set the alarm early enough to allow a sense of luxury in waking up slowly. This whole business of awakening is worth looking into, because in most cases it has a lot to do with one's whole behaviour pattern. Not wanting to wake up is often connected with not wanting to face certain aspects of life, which in the case of a violinist often means not wanting to face the violin. But if practising becomes a pleasurable, creative activity, it will tend to arouse a feeling of ease and anticipation in one's moments of 'coming to'.

Yoga and meditation are in great vogue these days. And there is no denying that they are wonderful antidotes to the speed and pressure one is exposed to. Menuhin devotes a whole chapter to breathing, posture, balancing and other yoga exercises in his book *Six Lessons with Yehudi Menuhin.** In fact, in his acknowledgements he mentions that sometimes he thinks his best violin teacher was his yoga guru. These exercises are described with marvellous insight, and players would be well advised to follow them.

*Faber Music Ltd., London, 1971.

126

The danger is that unless the directions are carefully followed (especially those concerning breathing) and unless one understands the philosophy that go with these exercises in general and with meditation in particular, yoga can do more harm than good. For those people who do not have the time or inclination to go into the mysteries of yoga, a few simple physical exercises (such as touching the toes, swinging the arms, etc.), will help to tone up the circulation as long as they are done every morning. Also a quiet leisurely breakfast, with a sense of luxury and pleasure (in being alive) is more important than one tends to realize.

After all, each morning is a little bit like being born anew and as there is no greater gift in life than life itself, it is a good thing to allow time for a conscious feeling of appreciation of this fact.

We are much more aware of the importance attached to wholesome food, to a well-balanced diet, than we have ever been before. One does not have to have ten bottles of vitamins and a shelf full of 'health foods' to realize how important an energy-giving diet is to one's health in general and to violin playing in particular.

So physical exercises, wholesome food and leisurely breakfasts are as important to good practising as is the practising itself. Comfortable clothes, a well-lit, pleasantly arranged room, however small (even if it is only a corner of a room) will all help to establish a sense of physical and mental well-being, and a sense of pleasurable anticipation for the beginning of the day's work.

Now the importance of total motion and balance with inside-outward energy impulses have been underlined all through this book. For it cannot be emphasized enough that the root of most problems concerning stage fright lies in forced and faulty physical actions. The problems of the mental attitudes often arise merely as a result of physical distortions. So the training is in three stages. I have found over and over again that *the first step is always to know what to do in order to release the physical blockages. The second step is to be able to apply constructive and positive mental attitudes. When these two are properly integrated the third step is to eliminate the 'self' by dissolving it into a free-flowing musical communication.*

It cannot be underlined enough that if practising is based on the principles of co-ordination and the interplay of balances, one hour can achieve better results than six hours of mechanical practising could ever do. And as time is a very scarce and precious commodity for many players, this is a most important point. Because, if a player feels he is developing in spite of the shortage of time spent at practising, frustrations and guilt will slowly disappear (see *A New Approach to Violin Playing*, pp. 61, 66 and 67).

In fact, although the actual time of practising at home may sometimes have to be reduced to the bare minimum, in a sense one does not cease to practise all day long. For, if one is aware of the principles of motion and balance, one's practising goes on while teaching or while playing in an orchestra. The act of applying these principles to pupils of all standards throughout the day is as good as if one applied them to oneself. For seeing results will certainly help reduce any subconscious resistance one may have had to them in one's own playing.

Equally, if one knows what sort of movements will prevent a backache when playing in an orchestra and what sort of motivation will release a shift, or co-ordinate a fast passage, the application of these measures will prove the most useful practise of the whole day's work; because exactly the same movements and thoughts will be needed for solo playing as well.

Also, if the suggestions for memorizing are carried out (see pp. 93-96) the practising of concertos can be easily done on buses, in trains, in rehearsal intervals, etc.

Reducing the actual hours of physical practise does not mean reducing the actual time of work spent in music-making in the form of creative activity.

It is most important to understand that this kind of work forms a continuous development and that it should never be looked upon as leading up to the achievement of one particular performance.

A definite order is essential in the programme of practising which covers the basic problems, even though the over-all time of practising is no more than twenty minutes or half an hour, as long as it is done (as it was pointed out before) first thing in the morning. Reduced to the bare minimum the order can go something like this:

1. The stance with the rhythmic pulse and singing (p. 19), and the exercises for the elimination of the violin hold (pp.

20-27) and the elimination of the bow hold (pp. 28-31) are basic essentials.

2. Correctly applied lower half, upper half and long open string strokes will help establish the fundamental balances in all the other strokes as well (pp. 32-38).

3. One of the four exercises set out in *A New Approach to Violin Playing*, on p. 34, will help to establish the search for overtones, but only if they are sung and mimed first. Play the first exercise one day, the second another day, the third the following day, etc., always in a different key.

4. The special 'silent' exercises for the thumb will help release tensions in the high positions (pp. 55-57).

5. The exercises for thirds and octaves set out in *A New Approach to Violin Playing* (pp. 46-47) combined with the left-hand finger action set out in this book (pp. 43-47) and with the fourth-finger exercises (pp. 49-50) also in this book, will help to develop elasticity and suppleness in the left hand action.

6. One exercise of the shift in *A New Approach to Violin Playing* (p. 44)—varying the fingers and the string each day—will help to give security when changing positions.

7. One three-octave scale played on one bow, stopping between each triplet as outlined in this book on p. 89, will help develop the left-hand lead in fast playing, and so will one line a day of Kreutzer No. 2, or a similar type of study.

End the practise with a few lines of your own choice of unaccompanied Bach, or a few lines from a concerto, or with a short piece. Apply the same principles of motion and balance as when playing scales and exercises.

The following exercises are set out with four hours of practising time in mind, which are to be divided into four separate hours. But it is important to understand that this is meant to be only a general outline and guide. The player is to use it with a great deal of elasticity, according to his own needs.

1. Exercises for the release of tensions with the rhythmic pulse, and singing (p. 19).

Apply these to an octave scale and then one or two (or more if necessary) troublesome phrases in any given piece you are working on, but never do more than one phrase at a time, and do not play these phrases on the violin yet.

2. Exercises for the release of tensions in the violin hold (pp. 22-27).

3. Exercises for the release of tensions in the bow hold and bowing arm (pp. 30-38).

The strokes are to be practised on the open strings—first in the lower half of the bow, then in the upper half. Continue with long strokes to the count of ten, then fifteen, going on up to twenty. Never play more than four strokes at a time of any of these exercises. Stop after four strokes, and re-think and re-check the salient points concerning the weight adjustments between the bow and the arm. Then start afresh on another string. The goal is to establish the fundamental balances, which then will ensure a self-propelled bowing arm in all other strokes as well.

4. Exercises for the release of tensions in the left-hand action (pp. 45-47).

Follow this with the four exercises given in *A New Approach to Violin Playing* (pp. 34, 35) in the first position. Pay special attention to the release of tensions concerning the fourth finger outlined in this book on pp. 48-50. Combine these exercises with ear training (p. 73). Singing the notes beforehand (with their note names) and saying them aloud while playing is one of the most important parts of all these exercises presented here. See the significance of identification as the central point of co-ordination (p. 81).

5. Exercises for the release of tensions in the high positions (pp. 55-57, 60-61).

Take out the four exercises given in *A New Approach to Violin Playing* (pp. 37, 38), play them in a different high position each day, in the fifth position one day, in the sixth the following day, then the seventh the next day, etc. Make certain you apply the silent, swinging-thumb exercises outlined in this book on pp. 55-56. Also make sure you revise the exercises given for the release of tensions in the violin hold. Continue after these exercises with those in Sevcik Op. 1, No. 2 in the fourth, fifth, sixth and seventh positions. Be aware of the dramatic quality of the intervals in these exercises and make the left hand responsible for realizing them.

6. Exercises for the release of tensions in the shifts (pp. 65-67). Continue with the exercises given in *A New Approach to Violin Playing* (pp. 42, 43) and with the exercises of Sevcik, Op. 8. When playing the Sevcik exercises, divide the bowing into four strokes in every bar. Play these exercises very slowly and make certain that the rhythmic pulse is well established (the quaver pulse if you play it slowly with the inner semi-quaver pulse) and that the left hand learns to swing into the position carried by the rhythmic pulse—instead of the vertical 'hopping' of the fingers on the string. Combine these exercises with studies like Fiorillo No. 25, Dont No. 15, Kreutzer No. 11.

7. Scales

Play one scale a day in the major, minor order, i.e. start with C major, go on to A minor, then G major, E minor, D major, B minor, etc., until you reach D♯ minor. Repeat F♯ major again but as G♭ major this time, then E♭ minor, D♭ major, B♭ minor, etc., until you reach C major. Then start the cycle again. I find Carl Flesch's scale book excellent and it is well worth working through it. Include the arpeggios, dominant 7th, diminished 7th, chromatics, broken thirds, scales, double stops and scales on the same string. When practising the three-octave scale slur only three notes to a bow first (one triplet) then six notes (two triplets) then twelve notes (four triplets). Play the three-octave scale going up on one stroke and coming down on another. First say each triplet rapidly, then play it. Stop between each triplet to have time to collect your thoughts, before saying the names of the notes. Then start on the top note of the scale and come down one stroke and go up on another, applying the same method as before. Equally, the arpeggios and diminished and dominant seventh are to be played in groups first. Also it is advisable to take the shifts out of context both in the scales and in the arpeggios and apply the same measures as before with the exercises for the shifts on pp. 65-67. However, it is important to play each exercise outlined above only once. Do not repeat automatically. Instead, if you feel any tensions building up, stop at once. Note where the tensions are. Re-think that bit of the music you happen to be playing, in the light of the instructions outlined in this book concerning those particular blockages. Then, play it again applying these instructions.

8. Exercises for the release of tensions in fast playing (pp. 86-90.)

   Combine the 'grouping' exercises outlined for the scales with studies such as Mazas No. 5, No. 6, Fiorillo No. 11, No. 12, etc. Take out only two or three lines of these or similar studies at any given time. Always vary the lines. Revise the semi-quaver open-string bowing (p. 86). Make sure you release the bow hold and that there is total co-ordination in the right-arm movement, so that it can become a reflex action to the lead of the left hand.

9. Exercises for the release of tensions in double stops.

   Revise the exercises for the release of tensions in the left hand action (pp. 45-47) with special attention to the elasticity of the fourth finger (pp. 48-50). Apply these actions to the double stops exercises in *A New Approach to Violin Playing* (p. 46) and to the double stops in the scales. Divide them on the down stroke as if they were two separate notes slurred, and then play them together on the up stroke. Pay special heed to the release of the left thumb (pp. 43-47), to the slide of the fingertip, and curling of the finger joints (p. 45), especially when the double stops are in the high positions. Also check on the release of the bow hold (pp. 29-31), because double stops tend to arouse extra anxiety in the right fingers as well. Follow these up with studies like Kreutzer No. 34, No. 35, etc, and Dont No. 10, No. 16, etc. Play only a few lines of each study, varying the lines each day. Make certain you build up the double stops from the lower finger (not the lower note) especially when the notes are played together. It cannot be emphasized enough that the elasticity in the hand will depend on the tension-free fourth-finger action (pp. 48-50). Always combine practising the double stops with special fourth-finger exercises such as Kreutzer No. 12 and No. 27, or another similar study of your choice. A few lines of a Paganini Caprice is recommended for the combination of the principles of motion and balance in shifts, double stops and high positions as one co-ordinated action.

132

10. Bach Unaccompanied.

Work on two different types of movement, even if these two do not belong to the same partita or sonata. For example, the Prelude in the E Major Partita or the Presto in the G Minor Sonata could be combined with the semi-quaver studies in Mazas, Fiorillo, etc. (following the suggestions for the release of tensions in fast playing outlined in this book on pp. 86-90), while the Siciliano, also in the G Minor Sonata, or the Sarabande in the D Minor Partita could be combined with the double stop studies in Kreutzer, Dont, etc. But again, a few lines a day of each will suffice, as long as the lines are always varied. After the study of a number of small movements one is more ready to start on something like the Chaconne or one of the Fugues. But these should be learned in sections, combined with scale work and relevant studies. It is advisable to play some unaccompanied Bach every day, because of its completeness (its independence from the need of other instruments) and because of the sheer beauty and transcendental quality which cannot help but leave a mark on the player's musical development.

11. Concertos

In order to acquire a varied repertoire it is advisable to have in hand two contrasting concertos: a 'small' one, perhaps one by Mozart, or by Bach, etc., and a 'large' one, something perhaps by Tchaikovsky, Sibelius, Brahms, etc. These too are to be practised in sections and by singing, miming, etc.

If there are any difficulties, try to work out the causes (mostly) they involve the fourth-finger action, string crossings, shifts, high positions, or a stiff bowing arm, which cannot follow the lead of the left-hand action). Relate all the particular problems to a scale or a study, instead of repeating any given passage over and over again. Make certain you work from the score, and listen to as many recordings and interpretations of the particular concertos you are working on as you possibly can.

12. The small pieces.

One could finish practising with an encore piece or two. Pieces like Kreisler's *Liebesleid, Schön Rosmarin,* etc., are highly recommended, because these are really impossible to play with physical blockages and so they provide a proper ending to the time spent with the violin.

2. *Suggestions for examinations, auditions, competitions, performances*

In order to eliminate stage fright, it always helps when the pieces to be played for any of these occasions are prepared well in advance. They can then be put away to 'rest' for a month or so, during which time one is occupied with establishing the same kind of releases from physical and mental blockages through learning a much more advanced or seemingly difficult repertory. The object is to realize that once one acquires sufficient skill in the actual handling of the instrument without any physical or mental blockages, the playing of the violin itself never presents difficulties (just as it does not present any difficulties to the gypsy violinist).

The work lies in acquiring greater and greater co-ordination and greater and greater musical awareness and imagination.

It cannot be said often enough that this kind of work should never be associated with notions of perfection and accomplishments; instead it should be looked upon as a never-ending development. Therefore, it is advisable before an important event to learn to play something much more difficult than that which is required for the particular occasion. Then, about two weeks beforehand, return to the pieces that have been prepared for the performance. The rest from them will not only assure a maturing period, but the additional skill and assurance acquired in the interim will make these pieces seem much easier to play than before.

However, the most important thing is completely to eradicate the criterion of 'good' and 'bad'. The major point of practising is to learn how to play through the violin (not on it), how to re-create the music with ease and pleasure, and with a continuous feeling of 'giving'. If there is nobody to 'give' the music to while practising, learn to direct your playing at a chair, or a desk, but always channel the transmission into one definite direction through the left hand action so that when playing for an examiner, auditioner, or an audience, you create exactly the same reaction in yourself as when playing at home.

3. *The salient points in practising*

1. Good conditions, good light, good ventilation, proper room temperature, good blood circulation, wholesome food.

2. The elimination of the violin-hold and the elimination of the bow-hold.

3. The differentiation between organic and forced, artificial movements concerning violin playing.

4. The fusion of the movements of the 'soft', 'alive' and 'weightless' violin with one's own perpetual motion and balance.

5. An established routine in the order of practising based on the principles of the inside-outward rhythmic energy impulses, singing (with naming the notes), and miming.

6. The connection of the naming of the notes with the left-hand action to which the bow strokes act as reflex responses.

7. The sending of all music (including exercises, scales and studies) through the instrument, from the tailpiece through the scroll, that is from the body via the left arm and through the roots of the left fingers—with a definite directive to the listeners.

8. The replacement of the artificial, oscillated vibrato with the continuous search for the overtones. The realization that tone production, intonation and vibrato are one and the same thing.

9. The realization that the violin is only the means of conveying the music to one's listeners and that the process of continuous release from physical blockages applies to the playing of Bach, concertos, and smaller pieces as well as to the playing of exercises, scales and studies.

10. The difference between practising from which one expects technical results with constant self-challenges and practising based on continuous creative activities which by their self-assuring qualities will in time help the player to dissolve his 'self' into musical communication.

11. The realization that it is physically impossible to hear the quality of one's own sound accurately, and the learning of the difference between 'listening' and 'hearing'.
12. The process of 'giving', regardless of whether one is at home or in front of three thousand people in a concert hall.

It is most important to understand that stage fright is nothing more than the fear of not being able to control one's actions in front of people. Of course the reasons for this can be as many as there are people, because each individual is different from any other. It would be an impossible task to discuss all the reasons on paper. What this book hopes to do is to point out the causes which seem to be most common among players who suffer from stage fright, and to offer some tangible cures. However, as all these collated suggestions deal with the principles of motion and balance and total co-ordination, (of both mind and body) one hopes that they will help to eliminate individual fears as well.

Finally it seems to me that the only way one can end a work like this, which has involved so many players from so many parts of the world, is with a last reminder that violin playing is never difficult; it is either easy, or it is impossible. And no matter how varied our individual idiosyncrasies may be, there is one common denominator in us all—we are all musicians. Not for a moment should we forget what an exalted position that is and has been all through the centuries. For music with movement is not only the one universal language uniting all mankind but, to quote Yehudi Menuhin, "Man's ultimate leap, when approaching his God, is through his music."*

It is important to realize that our responsibility as musicians lies just in this—in the lifting up emotionally and aesthetically of all our listeners, regardless of whether they are examiners, auditioners, or members of an audience. If all our energies were channelled into giving people, through the medium of music, a deeper understanding of their own potential as part of the wonderful mysteries that the universe contains, we would not only do justice to ourselves as musicians, but stage fright would be banished from the face of this earth for ever.

*Theme and Variations, by Yehudi Menuhin, Heinemann, London, 1972.

136

Printed and bound in Great Britain by
Caligraving Limited Thetford Norfolk